ONLY ONE LIFE:

a Quaker's voyage

Alastair Heron

Published by Curlew Productions
Kelso, Scotland
1998

© *Alastair Heron*

May 1998
Published by Curlew Productions, Kelso TD5 8PD, Scotland

ISBN 1 900259 07 9

Cover design by David Woolgrove
Set in Adobe Garamond 11/13.2 and Ultimate fonts

Typesetting & design by Curlew Productions, Kelso TD5 8PD, Scotland
Printed by Kelso Graphics, Kelso TD5 7BH

To the whole family

and

all my friends,

named or not

Alastair Heron

Foreword

I am doing this because over the years a number of friends and former colleagues have asked me to. These requests were independent: none of those making them have ever met, and they live on three continents. My resistance held until my son and friend Keith added his request to the others – at which point I gave in. There are dangers in writing about oneself to which one must be alert. First, there is the obvious difficulty in trying to record events and personal experiences with some degree of objectivity: to steer between the Scylla of false modesty and the Charybdis of hidden fault and failure. Next comes the unreliability of human memory, in terms both of selectivity and of accuracy, which increases with advancing age. And finally, when setting down an account of certain experiences it is essential to be tender of the feelings and good name of those involved. This may preclude reference altogether.

Contents

'The progress of man depends both on

conserving and on exploring:

and any full incorporation of

that life which will serve man's

spiritual interests now,

must find place for both.'

Evelyn Underhill (1921)

1 Grounding and launching

This started with what I gather my parents did regard as a happy event in Edinburgh, on 10 October 1915, just ten days short of the first anniversary of their wedding in London, at the very beginning of the Great War [as it was called until the next one made it (rather inaccurately) into World War I]. My mother was a nurse, a member of what today we would see as a rather large family of eight. Her father was the head of the Central Telegraph Office in St Martin's–le–Grand, in the City of London — a very responsible job in those days. I have only very vague memories of either him or my grandmother: they lived in a relatively small terraced house in Mitcham Lane (at the Streatham end) in south–west London. Two of my mother's sisters died of tuberculosis when young women; the other two became nurses as she did. Her three brothers were all caught up by the war, but survived — though the one (Dick) who had emigrated to Australia was very badly wounded in Gallipoli with the Anzacs, and never had an ordinary job again. Fortunately for him, the Australian provisions for disabled ex–Servicemen were very much better than those here in Britain. I never met him, but did meet Charlie in London and also made a trip across to Belfast to see Will, his wife and my two cousins.

Alastair, aged two years

My father was like myself born in Edinburgh, and although brought up in very comfortable circumstances, had anything but a happy early life. His mother was a Carnegie from Kirriemuir, about 30 miles northwest of Perth, and his father Alexander Heron was from nearby Blairgowrie. I never heard of Ellen Carnegie having any employment, and it is likely that she was married "straight from home". My grandfather was a Solicitor to the

Supreme Court in Scotland, and in due course he became the Secretary to the Merchant Company of Edinburgh, of which body he wrote the history. It seems that he was a stern man who knew his mind and was accustomed to be heard, and agreed with. My father said that his mother did stand up for him, but found this difficult and learned not to push matters too far with her husband. It is worth noting that my father spent his first 14 years in a combination of the late Victorian era with the Calvinism of the Church of Scotland. As an only child in such a setting, he probably did not have either an easy or a particularly happy childhood.

In later years I felt it necessary to take some of his claimed experiences with the proverbial pinch of salt, but I do not doubt that his determination not to follow his father into the legal profession was very real. At one point — most probably when he was about 17 — he pursued his true interests in a very practical way by signing–on as a prospective engineering apprentice for a trial voyage with a Leith–based shipping line. His father promptly used his Merchant Company connections and influence to have him sent back home — to what must have been an awesome confrontation between father and son. The latter actually managed to make his case (perhaps with the support of his more understanding mother) and was allowed to enter the University of Edinburgh to study engineering. This, by the way, followed what seems to have been a very successful 13 years (the whole of his schooling) at George Watson's College, one of the Merchant Company's clutch of top–class day–schools in Edinburgh. By the time he got to the university, he was apparently a reasonable flyweight boxer and in the first XV at rugby. While still at university he played in a trials match for the Scotland side, but came off the field concussed from an accidental kick to the head, and did not play at that level again. But in his early 40s he tried to get the 'English' game of rugby started again in Montreal, and refereed regularly for some years.

I did not find out until I was about 17 — and then from my mother in less than happy circumstances — that he apparently enjoyed the sporting and social life at the university rather too much, with the result that he did not pass his BSc finals. At some point — most probably in his early 30s — he obtained his AMIMechE. On the outbreak of war in 1914 he was commissioned second lieutenant in the Royal Garrison Artillery, and was posted to the Firth of Forth coastal defences. In 1917 or 1918 he was retired from the army on medical grounds [they called the condition neuraesthenia in those days], and went to the Ministry of Munitions (under Lloyd George). His father died before the war, and his mother during it, so by 1919 he had inherited not riches, but a tidy sum. This my parents were apparently quite unable to use wisely, as a few examples will demonstrate later, and it is sad to record that the only enduring outcome was that it made both of them somewhat snobbish.

On the move

At the beginning of the war, my mother was a theatre sister in one of the London teaching hospitals. After her marriage (which then and for the next more than thirty years made her unacceptable in hospital nursing), she was twice the matron of her own private nursing home, but although I gathered that she had the respect of the physicians and surgeons who sent their patients to her, she was prevented from making either of them a long–term success, simply because my father on both occasions moved off. On the first occasion, in 1920, we all went over to Canada via the eastern USA, where my father worked on the Welland Canal, to connect Lakes Ontario and Erie — and by so doing to foreshadow the eventual St Lawrence Waterway, which enabled seagoing vessels to proceed beyond Montreal right through to Lake Superior at the head of the Great Lakes. At the beginning of that first trip to North America, I remember vividly a short stay in what I later found was probably Scranton, Pennsylvania, because the railroad ran right through the centre of the town, with streets and shops on either side. It was certainly a sight (and sound, with the big bell on the huge locomotive) for a little boy of just five!

We lived in St Catherine's, Ontario and so were close to the Niagara fruit belt where in late summer it was quite in order to help oneself to a *few* peaches. My other remembered experience was of a different order altogether. One day my mother and I were down on the Lake Ontario beach, when I caught sight of some people having plenty of fun about a hundred yards out. So 5-year–old simply set off to join them — and disappeared under the waves while mother was in conversation with another woman. Apparently a man saw me do so, and ploughed his way out to where I was, to haul me up by my hair. It was a near thing, and one natural result was a fear of the water which was not overcome for many years.

Having gone out (probably from Southampton) to New York, we returned from Montreal to Liverpool, where my father must either have had a job waiting for him, or found one immediately on our arrival. As a result, I went to my first school — a small private one in Bootle — at the age of six. From its term report, it seems that with two notable exceptions a good start was made. The exceptions were remarkably predictive: for singing, 'Fair attempt'; and for drawing 'Good attempt'!

So what can I remember, with enough confidence to record, about these early years? My earliest memory of an 'event' goes back to three or four. My parents had apparently given me a pedal motor–car [probably for one of those birthdays], and I was out near the house with it. Some larger boys, who could have been anything from five to eight or nine years old, wanted a ride. Possessive though unlikely to have appeared fierce, I must have refused — so they simply dragged me out of it and took their 'rides'. I have no idea what happened after that, but would hazard a guess that I bawled my head off and rushed back into the house!

Life at home

Some of my other recollections have already been picked up as we went along, so a few lines are in order about my home life. I became aware in the Tulse Hill nursing home that my parents both seemed prone to getting into tempers, in my father's case with my mother and in her case with both him and her sister Molly, who I think lived there and worked as a nurse. One day he disappeared, and it was several months before I was told that he had been located in Newcastle–upon–Tyne, where he had got an engineering job. By then it was clear to me that he had not just 'changed jobs again', but had gone off to have a more peaceful existence. So that explains the move to Newcastle [my principal memory is that of a typical seven–year–old: the big steam locomotive crossing the Tyne rail bridge into Newcastle Station!].

There we lived in a small house in Gosforth, with a bit of garden at the front, yard at the back. After some time, we acquired a lodger called Leonard, who was in his twenties. He had a bicycle, and took me on the top bar of the frame [sitting sideways, no seat] on little outings. The best of these were to the sea at Whitley Bay. Unfortunately, he turned out to be what I now know as a paederast, and so provided me at first hand with clear evidence that a seven–year–old can be innocent, in the sense of naive. His activities were fairly limited, fortunately for me, and any danger that he might have taken things further was averted by my father 'catching on', with the resulting instant departure of the said Leonard. I was questioned and then warned of the dangers, though in oblique terms associated with sinful practices. Looking back, I am grateful that so strict — and in many other ways stern and rigid – a man as my father handled the episode in the way he did.

He was always yearning to get back to his native Edinburgh, an aim furthered by my mother's frequently outspoken convictions that he could and should make use of his 'connections' there. These in fact were limited to one or two retired colleagues of his father, and a few school or university acquaintances. Father was like myself an only child, with the result that neither he nor I had many Scottish relatives. However, he did manage it and north we went in September 1923. At first we lived in a large house down in the New Town, with two of my father's aunts, and then in a flat at the top of the building in George Street belonging to a well–known firm of auctioneers, Lyon and Turnbull. Quite often on my return from school about 4.00 o'clock, I would join my mother down there: she was quite a connoisseur, though rarely able to buy anything, and I learned a good deal about the 'tricks of the trade' [which turned out to be useful much later.].

My father enjoyed messing about with the very early 'crystal sets', using headphones which you put in a pudding bowl to amplify the thin sound! I put my young foot in it one day, when he was trying to sell one of these and claiming that we were listening to 2LO (London): I blurted out 'No — that's the Edinburgh relay station'. He gave me an almighty telling–off afterwards, the more because Galileo–like I insisted that I had been right! I was very lucky to escape a stroke or two of the tawse – the traditional Scottish implement of summary punishment, used at home and in school until the 1980s, applied to the hand.

But this was the beginning of the really difficult years, as my mother became more and more likely to 'take a drink or two, or three', and the rows between her and my father became more frequent. Of course I didn't know it then, but it must have been near the beginning of her menopause. And she told me only a very few years later how depressed she had been, from an early stage in her marriage, by the realisation that she was unlikely to have any more children. Some at least of the tension between them must have been due to her belief — whether well-founded or not — that my father had become impotent.

One early evening, I simply fled when they were having a row, and pelted down the hill to my great-aunts (and middle-teens second cousin), who took me in for the night. This was temporarily salutory for my parents, and things quietened down for some time. Not long afterwards — and I never knew or have forgotten — my father either fell out with his employers, or simply got itchy feet, and the decision was taken to emigrate to Canada. Wisely, they decided to leave me to have a second year at my school before bringing me out to join them.

We had moved to Edinburgh in time for me to be enrolled in my father's old school, where in two sessions a sound basis was laid for my formal education. At that time George Watson's College was still on its original site on the city side of The Links, next door to the Royal Infirmary, where its place was taken later by the Simpson Maternity Wing. It was normal for most of us in my age-group to walk to and from school, unless the weather was really bad, when one rode on the famous (because good) Edinburgh trams. This is probably the point at which to note that from my first school to my last, I was always the smallest member of my class. This combined uncomfortably with also being one of the top three performers academically, and being a non-starter in the usual sports because of my size and lack of weight. Some bullying was probably inevitable, and was never wholly absent.

Everybody had to turn out for rugby [in a school famous for its contributions to the Scottish sides], but I didn't have my father's gift for it and doubt if I'd have even made my little mark as a fly-half! In my second year [after they had gone to Canada], I contracted German measles and went straight into the local infectious diseases hospital, where (unsurprisingly) I picked up whooping cough, and so had a prolonged stay. It says a good deal for the school and my teachers that I was not allowed to slip back in my lessons, and so escaped the all-too-frequent onset of problems with number, arising directly from 'getting behind' with no immediate remedial action. But overall, I remember being quite happy during that year, in which by the way I attended regularly both church and Sunday School at the Church of Scotland in Morningside, thus getting a good grounding in Bible knowledge, as well as much friendliness and warmth. I have no recollection of any narrowness, of the kind sometimes reported by those exposed to a potentially Calvinistic emphasis in the 'Kirk' of John Knox.

So I had a year's holiday from the domestic stresses, and enjoyed life probably more than was to be the case for a long time thereafter. Quite irrationally, I also became a Scot without noticing it: even fifty years later, never having lived again in my native country, I was to experience a very real sense of just 'feeling something was different' when I crossed the Border from England — for example, in the sleeping car, waking for my breakfast.

Off to Canada

In the late summer of 1925 my parents arranged for me to join them in Montreal. This involved being a passenger from Leith in a cargo ship called the *Cairnross*, in the care of the Captain. As in practice this care was delegated to the bo'sun, young Alastair had a much more interesting voyage than would have been the case on a liner. There was a seemingly endless number of small, undemanding tasks to be performed all over the ship, and one major one: to re–paint in black all the bollards, capstans and similar lumps of cast iron which cluttered the deck–space of such a vessel. The last stage of the voyage was of course the nearly 1000 miles up the St Lawrence River from the Atlantic Ocean to Montreal, then the largest inland seaport in the world. It was the total impression that lasted in the memory: details like the city and ramparts of Quebec did not register on the little traveller.

But the first sight of Montreal did register, as the ship edged its way to the quayside – despite the fact that two crushed fingers were causing a fair amount of pain at the time.

Steel Cross on Mont Royal

Behind the city — then with but a couple of buildings more than 20 floors in height – rose Mont Royal, tree–covered and with its famous lattice–steel cross at the summit. My parents were there to meet me, and off we went to the boarding–house in which they were staying. The outstanding feature of my first meal was corn–on–the–cob with lots of butter! Within a month we had moved into a nearby apartment–house [= block of flats] in the City of Westmount (which is surrounded by the larger City of Montreal).

Two more schools

Westmount had four elementary schools, of which the nearest [King's School] was about 15 minutes walk away, across the grass area in front of the High School, adjacent to Westmount Park. Fortunately I liked the Principal and my class teacher, which made it easier to start in an unfamiliar system — and nearly at the top end, with only two school years to go before high school. It very soon became obvious that my time at Watson's in Edinburgh had provided a sound basis, giving me some advantage over the others. When combined with my small stature, preventing me from doing well at games, that was no way to win general acceptance!

Alastair in a kilt

The first disaster took place quite soon. One Saturday afternoon, my mother decided that we would go for a walk in the park — but also that I should wear the kilt! My protests were futile, and off we went. It was bad enough to be looked at all the time, and to know that comments were being made, but worse was in store. An 'American–type' rugby match between the High School and some visiting team from Montreal was under way, with quite a crowd milling around the touch–lines. An unexpected end–run resulted in someone being bundled into touch — and in my being knocked over! I wasn't hurt, only mortified because of the kilt, but even then I could have coped had I been on my own. But my mother characteristically made a big fuss about it instead of just quietly walking away. One sad consequence was my firm refusal ever to wear the kilt again.

The Canadian winter soon arrived, and with it the open–air skating rinks, one for the ice–hockey and the other for pleasure skating generally. I 'found my feet' on the ice–skates fairly quickly [though I was never expert], but ice–hockey was a non–starter simply because of my size: I was just slammed into the boundary boards! Sometime during the winter, some of the big boys in my class decided to have some fun with me on my way home, by burying me up to my neck in deep snow. The result was a week off school to recover from exposure. When I went back, I had the sense not to say anything, but of course hadn't reckoned with mother. She turned up outside the school door that afternoon as we all poured out, and told all and sundry what she thought of bullies who would bury a smaller boy in snow. Bad enough, you might say – but then she added as her parting shot 'He's got more sense in his little finger than some of you have in your whole bodies!'.

It was that episode, however, that led to the first real friendship of my life. One of my classmates took me under his wing from then on, and it made all the difference. This was Bob Logan, with whom I am still in touch. His family were from Ireland, where his father had worked for the railways as a senior engineer. Our new friendship was put to the test much sooner than either of us could have suspected: within a year my father's job came to an end [I never heard why] and we had to leave our Westmount apartment. It seems that the funds ran out about then, so we had to move [just] into the French area of Montreal to find a cheaper dwelling. Here it must be explained that Montreal was effectively divided from north to south by Rue St Denys: all east/west streets crossing St Denys are numbered east and west from it. Almost everything west was Anglophone, and everything east Francophone.

I remember that our flat was at the top [second floor], and very cold. In Montreal [and Westmount] the equivalent of the British 'semi–detached' house was the duplex – one on top of the other. Similarly, our terraced houses were 'stacked', with a ground floor flat surmounted by two others, the entrance doors of which were side by side at first–floor level, at the top of straight outside flights of steps. The latter were a small source of income for boys after each snowfall in winter – 10 cents for clearing one flight, which as I recall took half–an–hour when there was a foot of snow or more, all the way up. While we're at it: the other main earnings came from delivering groceries, on a sled in

Montreal 'duplex' flats with outside stairs

winter, and an oblong cart with four wheels called a 'roller coaster' the rest of the year. By the way, the pair of doors at the first–floor level provided occasional 'sport' when bored: you just balanced the empty milk bottles on the sloped draught–excluding strip of the door leading to the inside staircase of the *upper* flat, pressed the bell, and raced away to the nearest out–of–sight vantage point to await results. Oddly enough, the bottles rarely broke, just producing a very satisfying clatter!

My father decided to buy and instal a 'Quebec heater', with nine–inch diameter flue pipes which had to be suspended from the ceiling all the way to the vent in the back wall. This ancestor of the modern slow–combustion stove was able to burn coal, coke or wood – but my father, being a Scot in more than one sense of the term, decided to locate a supply of peat which was much cheaper. It burned very well and provided plenty of heat – but deposited all its water content along the length of the overhead flue pipes, with the consequent steady drip of oily brown water under every joint. This not only kept us all pretty busy and made us extinguish the heater, but elicited some understandably acid comment from my mother, still smarting from the loss of our centrally–heated Westmount apartment.

I now found myself coming mid–session into the nearest elementary school, which happened to be in the adjoining Anglophone area with a predominantly Jewish population. This was of course my last session before hoping to go on to high school, so I just had to do the best that I could with changes of curriculum and approach. I also had to adjust to co–education — but found this not too difficult largely because most of the girls were friendly. In my second [and last] term there, we had a prize–essay competition on the subject of famous composers. (I certainly did not then realise how this was related to the universal interest — and ability — of Jewish people in classical music).

The brightest girl in my class chose Mozart, and I chose Beethoven though I cannot remember why! She came first and I came second.

The High School years

This brings the story to the matter of secondary education in Montreal in 1927. For educational purposes, the city was divided between Catholic and Protestant boards of school commissioners. There were several Protestant high schools, including the one in the mainly Jewish area, but the recognised 'plum' was the pair of schools near McGill University in the city centre. These — housed in a large cream–coloured building in the shape of a letter **H**, then only a few years old, were The High School of Montreal [for boys] and The High School for Girls. Had I spent the *whole* of my last year in my elementary school after leaving Westmount's jurisdiction, I would have been awarded a government scholarship covering the (then) four years of high school, because I ended with third place in my class. But I was not eligible, and the money for even the first year's fees and the cost of textbooks simply wasn't available.

My mother then showed her undoubted mettle, and took me down to be interviewed by the Rector of the High School of Montreal. This at the time was a fatherly and scholarly man called Dr. Gemmell. He looked at my

The High School of Montreal

Watson's, King's and current reports, heard my mother out, asked me a few questions – and said [I can almost hear him still] 'We shall be glad to have Alastair in the High School — I am sure that he will do well'. We would have gone home in complete triumph, but for the apparently insoluble financial problem. My father had a job of some sort, but it was not well–paid and I am almost certain we were in debt.

At the end of the next day, my mother sat down with me and said 'You will go to the High School: I have sold my rings for enough money to pay this year's fees and to buy your books. That is all I can do — the rest is up to you: as you know, it means that you will have to win a scholarship at the end of every year in order to stay on'. Yes, I did know that.

Here I want to bring in a story from my mother's days as a young probationer (now termed student) nurse in London, around 1905. Apparently she was both high–spirited and strong–willed, and did not accommodate readily to the extremely strict discipline inherited from Florence Nightingale. The probationer nurses of course lived in, and had to obtain signed passes to go out for the evening when off–duty – for example to a medical–school dance. Usually they had to be back by a stated hour such as 11 p.m. On one occasion, my mother didn't make it, so decided to go over the wall, and in through an accessible window. Unfortunately she chose the wrong window: that of an off–duty day sister. The penalty was extreme: she was dismissed from the hospital, and had to continue her training at another less prestigious hospital prepared to accept her. This tale may be surprisingly familiar to some readers, since it corresponds quite closely with an episode in the well–known film *Doctor in the House*, starring James Robertson Justice, around fifty years later!

During my first year, father got a better job and we moved to an apartment in the Jewish area, but very near the north–eastern slopes of Mont Royal — the 750–foot Mountain around which Montreal and other smaller cities like Westmount and Outremont are clustered. And in my entry class I met my second close friend, Sam Hershenkopf, who lived a few streets away from us. His father a small, alert and friendly man, was a cobbler and bootmaker from the Ukraine, who had emigrated to Canada before the 1914-1918 war. He had a little shop where Sam helped after school [he made his own shoes from the age of eleven], and before long I was almost part of the family. This friendship and acceptance meant a great deal to me, One direct result for my broader education for life was my unconscious appreciation of another culture, and of another faith (though I already knew from Sunday school back in Edinburgh that Jesus was a Jew).

My four years in high school were a rich mixture — of what for me was I suppose the 'good things' and the 'not–so–good', or 'bad' things. It was soon apparent that the combination of being the smallest boy in the class with being both bright and [of necessity] extremely hard–working, was not the best way to become popular. Fortunately for me, the school, already about 90 years old, had an ethos based on tradition, fortified by the calibre of the Rector — and by a general background of parental support, despite the lack of a parent–teacher association. So although I did get a bit of bullying, it never got out–of–hand and I learned how to survive. Probably unfortunately for my later adult personality (and for those who had to put up with it), I quickly learned also how to use my tongue to speak up for myself – and sometimes to gain respect from bigger boys just because I did.

Most team sport was out of the question: when I turned out for junior ice-hockey, as usual I was simply brushed aside or slammed into the side–boards of the rink. So I decided to go for solo activities, which in the end turned out to be ski–ing and small–bore rifle shooting. At the former, I became competent enough to enjoy myself and to go out with the others, though never big and fast enough to gain a team place. The rifle shooting was a different story altogether, which had a humorous beginning. When in my first term I joined the school cadet corps, it wasn't long before the annual search for potential 'shots' began. So I turned up after school [at its own indoor rifle–range!] and took my turn down on the mat. Having shortened the sling as fully as possible on the rifle, I then wrapped it round my left arm as tightly as I could, and spread myself out, rifle in position. Then I heard the voice [though I could not see more than the legs] of the master in charge of the cadet corps: 'Heron, you will never be able to shoot properly like that!' To this I replied respectfully 'It's the only way I *can* manage, sir'. So my line of six boys down on the mat was given its instructions, and told to go ahead with our ten shots at the target, 25 yards away. All my shots hit the target somewhere within the range of concentric circles, and several were in or touching the 'bull'. Comment from Mr Heslam [deadpan voice]: 'Quite good, Heron'. That launched me into a series of school teams, ultimately to winning the outdoor small–bore rapid–fire medal at the Canadian equivalent of the British Bisley.

In the cadet corps during my four high school years I was successively private, corporal, sergeant and lieutenant — in each case the shortest in living memory. I qualified in all branches of military signalling, and enjoyed everything we did. Back to the classroom now: each year I duly won the scholarship needed to keep me going – and was taken under the wing of the school librarian. One of the first high schools in Canada to have both a proper library and a trained full–time librarian in its new 1920s building next door to McGill University, it also had a theatre–equipped auditorium and an indoor heated swimming pool. When I got to Britain in 1934, I was amazed to discover that even the most modern grammar–school buildings had nothing to compare with this –

The smallest ever lieutenant (1931)

and certainly no full–time trained librarians! So Miss Charlotte Houston taught me how to respect and use books and libraries, and introduced me gently to extra–curricular browsing that enlarged my horizons. In later years, I kept in touch with her by post right up to her death in the early 1950s, just too soon for me to see her again when at last I got back to Montreal in 1954. My wife Margaret and I visited her sister in 1969, on M's first trip to Canada.

The High School of Montreal [and the High School for Girls, occupying the other half of the H–shaped building, with an invisible line across the corridor on each floor!], were the pinnacle of the Protestant Board of School Commissioners' educational provision for the City of Montreal. In those days, the Anglophone population was dominant: almost all the Francophones were

Roman Catholic, while the Anglophones were a religious mixture in which Protestants were the great majority, with Jewish people in second place. In my class, we always had one or two Protestant French–Canadians, and no doubt the same was true in the main RC high schools the other way round. We also had an ethnic mixture which all of us took for granted: in my class boys of Chinese, Portuguese, and Caribbean mixed–blood origins, and of course those then called 'coloured' who would now wish to be known as 'black'. Most of these boys came from families that had migrated from or through the USA and had become Canadians. For me, this was the foundation of my adult complete acceptance of ethnic equality, for which foundation I have always been grateful.

Although our two High Schools were separate, we were actively encouraged to mix socially through the use of the theatre (mostly in the Shakespeare plays currently in the curriculum.), and in the Sixth Form at joint dances. During school hours the girls all wore 'sailor–suit' blouses and navy skirts, but in the boys school we had no uniform. Of course we all dressed–up for the dances, which on my first occasion was quite a revelation. For my first dance, it was even more so, because the girl from their Sixth Form who was asked by the Lady Principal to invite me onto the floor was about a foot taller! I think many of the girls felt more than a little sorry for me, as I was so small, and did their best (then and later — yes, I kept going to the dances each term) to put me more at my ease. Later on, after leaving school, I went to dances with my friend Sam Hershenkopf and his girlfriend: they were such experts that on occasion everybody would get off the dance floor just to watch them. But even they couldn't make me into a passable ballroom dancer — except in the slow waltz, of which there were not enough for me! But I valued their friendship and down–to–earth caring.

My first job

I graduated from high school in June 1931, with the equivalent of a School Certificate in England, good enough to give me matriculation to McGill University. But I was both too young [under 16] and without the funds, so was lucky to get a job as an office–boy in the head office of an oil company, located in the first of Montreal's 'skyscrapers' [20 stories!], the Royal Bank of Canada Building. One of the vice–presidents of this company was the

Canadian flying 'ace' of the 1914–18 war, Colonel William Avery Bishop, VC DSO etc.. On a never–to –be–forgotten day, he paused by my desk in reception, and said 'I hear you are interested in flying – would you like to come with some of us this afternoon?'. We [including the office manager, my immediate boss] went out to the aerodrome at St Hubert, to take off in a very new Sikorsky amphibian, and then land on a stretch of the Ottawa River northwest of Montreal. There everybody [all male] stripped off, and we were disporting ourselves in the water when a car arrived with the ladies. So we all had to swim round to the other side of the hull, climb out and get dressed for the picnic. What a story to take back to my parents! [Yes — they *were* impressed].

A few months later, I made what proved to be a very stupid career decision, when on seeing a job advertised for a laboratory assistant in a firm of analytical chemists, I applied for and obtained it. The background was my great interest in chemistry at school, which came second only to my impossible ambition to be a surgeon. What I was too immature to realise was the difference in job security between my oil–company job and the new opening. A few months later, I was made redundant when the analytical chemists ran into financial difficulty, as a delayed result of the 'Great Depression' that started in 1929.

Unemployment in 'the Great Depression'

During the next three years, I was but one among millions of unemployed — and in Canada there was not even the British 'dole' for either my father or myself. He was unemployed in spells between temporary jobs: I later reckoned that I had anything between a few days and a few weeks in more than twenty different jobs. At times we were both unemployed simultaneously, which meant total reliance on the charitable organisations for help. Then I felt as long–term unemployed people always do: unwanted, 'superfluous to requirement', short on real hope. We had to move our dwelling–place [for betterment or by necessity for the worse] frequently: in my whole nine years in Montreal, the longest period under the same roof was about eighteen months or so. The low ebb was the day I watched the bailiffs take almost all our furniture off the removal van. But we were never actually homeless, so I don't know what that feels like.

In the winter, I usually went ski–ing on Mont Royal when the conditions were right; sometimes it was extremely cold, and I well remember the day when, with a clear blue sky and bright sunshine, the air temperature was minus 22F (equal to –30C). I was astonished to hear almost every word when two skiers spoke to one another, about 150 yards away across a ravine.

In the dark green 'dress uniform' of the Rifle Brigade (1934)

I was taught how to ride a bicycle by my friend Bob Logan, while we were both still at high school (he in Westmount of course), but did not acquire my own until I was nearly 17. (It had no gears, and a back–pedal hub brake, so I tried to avoid the urban slopes of Mont Royal!). In the summer of 1932 I cycled twelve miles each way each day to caddy on a golf course, usually getting up at 6.30 in the hope of putting in three 18–hole rounds. (At that time I was the only source of income). Following my father's example, I laid everything I earned on the table for my mother to use on our joint behalf. We had a small amount of agreed 'spending money', varying with our circumstances at the time. I joined a local Territorial regiment [the Victoria Rifles of Canada, attached to the Rifle Brigade] under age, where I could employ my cadet and shooting experience and skills to good advantage. In due course, I qualified as a Vickers machine–gunner and obtained my Sergeant's certificate [though not the actual rank]. My social life was obviously limited financially, but sometimes I had an evening out with Sam Hershenkopf and some former schoolmates. Oh, yes — I have forgotten to mention that about a year after leaving school, and when first unemployed, I grew five inches in twelve months! This happened when the family finances were very tight, so I had to watch my sleeves go up my wrists and my trousers up my ankles – and feel my toes get tighter in my shoes.

When I was jobless during the long months of the Montreal winter, I often read one book (from a lending library) every 24 hours – unless it was very long, as was the case with Boccaccio's *Decameron* and other classics. Around that time, I started to read one of my father's school prizes – a set of three Stoic classics: *The teachings of Epictetus, The meditations of Marcus Aurelius,* and *The Morals of Seneca.* I found the Stoic philosophy attractive and helpful, and in a limited way started trying to practise it. One basic tenet gripped me: concern yourself about those matters over which you may have some control, do not concern yourself about matters over which you can have no control.

Tourists, immigrants and emigrants

In the summer of 1933, I got a seasonal job as what they called a 'lecturer' with one of the two bus companies that ran two–hour sight–seeing tours of the city, and across the river (St Lawrence) to the 'Indian' Reservation. Most of the other lecturers (or 'spielers') rolled out a commentary (using a sort of trumpet – no electronic gadgetry in those days! — without too much concern about facts, but I suppose my educational privilege combined with my sense of integrity to make me want to do rather better than that. So I learned everything that I could about the buildings and places we passed on the city tour, as well as about the history of the city (founded in 1642 by the French explorer the Sieur de Maisonneuve). Most of our customers were from the USA, and sometimes one would express appreciation for what he might describe as 'a different quality of commentary from what he'd got used to'. Gradually it became obvious to my driver(s) that our average income from the tips was higher than that to which they were accustomed.

Most weekends, several coaches with attached trailers were sent to the main railway stations, and to the port, to convey passengers in each direction, with their luggage. As noted earlier, before the opening of the St Lawrence Seaway through a canal system by–passing the rapids above Montreal, it was the largest inland seaport in the world. The river was (and of course still is) closed by ice during the winter above the city of Quebec. The master of the first ocean–going ship to reach Montreal was each year awarded a special cane by the Port Authority [I don't know whether this practice has continued].

During the summers of 1933 and 1934, the people we took off the incoming liners from Britain and the Continent on Friday evenings were almost all from the Baltic states (Latvia etc), Poland, Hungary, and Czechoslovakia. They usually had the minimum of spoken English required for immigration, and were headed for the Prairie provinces of Alberta, Manitoba and Saskatchewan. When we went to the stations on Sundays to collect passengers for the same ships, almost all were British immigrants who were going back to unemployment and poverty in Britain: they had been unable to adapt to the rigours and hardships of new life in the West. In contrast, those from Continental Europe seemed to be able to 'make a go of it'. After the 1939–45 war, the same pattern recurred and was also was observed in Australia. My guess is that those from the Continental countries had 'burned their boats', so to speak — or felt strongly that they had done so.

Working my passage

This makes as good an introduction as any to the next change in my own circumstances: in early 1934 my parents decided that however bad the prospects were in Britain, they could not be any worse than in Montreal, and so felt they too should go back to 'the old country'. We had by then been living in the flat on the roof of a city–centre branch of the Bank of Toronto for about 18 months: my father was the uniformed 'messenger', and the caretaker of the building. So all three of us combined to do the cleaning and polishing. One of my tasks was to polish the big brass plates outside the front doors of the bank, at about 8.00 a.m. every morning. This was a sinecure in the summer, but a different matter altogether in the winter. I remember vividly the morning when the air temperature was –31 degrees Fahrenheit (–35C.): I couldn't polish the plates because the Brasso froze on my cloth immediately! [The coldest that I ever experienced was in my very early days in Montreal, when my father took me to Trois Rivieres (on the river about halfway to Quebec), where he had an engineering job for a time in a huge pulp/paper mill: it was –55F (–41C.)]

So it was decided that hard saving from our combined earnings would pay for a one–way ticket on a cargo boat for mother, but my father and I would have to hope for chances to work our passages to Britain. This would have been close to unrealistic, had not my father earned the respect of the Harbour

Master in the Port of Montreal, through his earlier readiness to take any work however unskilled or arduous. For example, I remember in mid–summer 1933 when he was unemployed, a ship came in needing work on its boilers. So that it could turn around quickly, this meant getting inside the boilers to hack the scale off the inside lining, before they had fully cooled after the fires had been drawn. My father was offered 72 hours work on this, and didn't hesitate. I can still see him coming home exhausted for a bath and sleep — and cannot forget the stink of stale sweat. While he slept, my mother washed his underclothes and overalls, and had them ready for him with his meal on awakening.

Back to Britain

S.S. Manchester Commerce

At the beginning of October 1934, about two weeks after my mother had set off for Britain, a chance turned up for both of us – remarkably on the same ship. The fourth engineer had gone straight into hospital on arrival, and one of the 'trimmers' in the 'black squad' had jumped ship and disappeared. The ship was the *Manchester Commerce*, of about 5000 tons, one of the many vessels of the Manchester Line. She was to call at Halifax for cargo (including apples) en route to Liverpool. Built to be oil–fired, she had been converted to use coal because, as a result of the depression, this had become very much cheaper than oil — and at that time there was too much coal in Britain that could not find a market. [shades of things to come!]

So the oil–tanks had become tall narrow coal–bunkers, which had to be kept full by the 'trimmers' at the top, working in a large horizontal bunker area, shovelling coal into iron wheelbarrows, which had to be run up a short plank over the lip of the former oil–tank, and tipped. I was the only pink–skinned member of the black squad (usually called Lascars) consisting of the firemen (below) and the trimmers at the top. In each watch there were four firemen and two trimmers. The first job of the trimmers when coming on duty at the beginning of the watch involved breaking up the slag and clinker that had collected on the actual fire–beds, using long–handled cast iron 'sledges'. With the fire–door open, and the fireman standing back while you did it, this was a tough hot job that had to be done quickly.

Although fairly strong, I was unused to this extreme physical work, but did my best and was encouraged by my trimmer mate and by the firemen. But the Second Engineer was a bullying type of man, who made a habit of coming through from the engine–room to stand over me and rant about my slowness. At the beginning of what was probably my fourth or fifth watch, he was doing this. Despite the noise and my physical efforts, I became aware that something was happening in the narrow strip behind the fires, where the firemen were standing back. I risked a quick glance, just in time to see the engineer leaving us — and one of the firemen standing with one of the heavy clinker–breaking 'sledges' in his hand, the other firemen tensely watching.

They all clapped me on the back and one of them said 'You won't have any more trouble from him!'. Up aloft, I asked my trimmer mate about it. 'Oh, they told him to leave you alone if he wanted to finish the voyage!' He then pointed out that if he had 'disappeared', they would all say that he had left the boiler–room area, not by returning to the engine–room, but by going up the vertical ladder which came out on the small deck around the funnel — and must have gone overboard accidentally. This was my introduction to a very different 'world' from that in which I had grown up.

On a quite different note, it is one of my precious memories that my mate was the first to wish me a happy birthday (19) in mid–Atlantic. And then there was the 'very lucky indeed' episode. We ran through some very rough weather in the north Atlantic, and wheeling a heavy load of coal up the plank and tipping it had to be neatly timed, as we pitched (fore and aft) or rolled (side to side), or corkscrewed (both together!). One watch, I misjudged and my loaded wheelbarrow shot out of my hands down onto the pile of coal, and I went with it. Very fortunately for me, I had the coal level high already, so only fell a few feet: but I might have broken an arm or fallen hard onto the end of a wheelbarrow handle. As I looked up, there was my mate – anxiety written all over his dark face – peering down at me. When we both realised that I had 'got away with it', we had a good laugh!

On arrival at Liverpool, my father and I were paid off, and sought a bed–and–breakfast to spend the night, before going on to London to join my mother. But before everything else, we went to the Public Baths where I soaked as much as possible of the coal dust out of my pores, then on to a huge meal. I was given a Merchant Navy discharge book, with my voyage and 'good conduct' signed for. So I could have gone to sea again later if I had wanted to (or needed to, more likely).

In London the three of us rented a small semi–basement flat just up the road from Brixton (later Lambeth) Town Hall. Mother was renewing contact with the surviving members of her family still in London: her brother Charlie, with his wife and my cousin Dick; and one sister (Molly) with whom my mother tended to have a rather combative relationship, often stormy. They were both experienced nurses of the tough pre–1914 training era, and equally sure that they were in the right about most things. Meanwhile, my father and I started job hunting: fortunately, he found something fairly soon (though I cannot recall what it was — or in fact what work he did during the 1934–1936 period in the London area).

I found nothing, not even as an office boy (too old at 19), nor in any analytical chemist firm that I approached. There was one high spot in that two months I spent in London: this was the day when Molly, my mother and I went to the West End, where we had lunch at a Lyons Corner House. These were huge very popular restaurants, at Marble Arch, Charing Cross and Leicester Square. (They all closed down during the 1950s or 60s, and both Londoners and visitors were the poorer for it, as compared with what progressively took their place). After lunch, we were walking across Leicester Square when I caught sight of the boards outside the old Leicester Square Theatre: 'Monte Carlo Ballet Russes'. I had never seen ballet but felt strongly drawn to this chance of experiencing it. Neither Molly nor my mother wanted to go, but I was firm and arranged to meet them later. I got a cheap seat in 'the gods' (the gallery), and far from ideal for ballet, in view of the steep angle down to the stage. But it was for me literally fantastic, unforgettable. The most vigorous part was the Polovtsian Dances from Borodin's opera 'Prince Igor'; the most beautiful all in white, but I don't remember the name of the ballet. The two principal ballerinas were Baronova and Tamara Toumanova, the latter already at my own age what I later learned to know as a 'prima ballerina assoluta'. So that is how ballet became important for me. Toumanova lived until 1996.

Into the Regular Army

As it became increasingly obvious that I was unlikely to get work in London, and with things at home in the little flat always likely to flare up, I suppose it was unsurprising that one morning I went up to Whitehall, and walked into the Central Recruiting Office of the Regular Army. A sergeant sat me down and took my particulars, then went on to mention what he thought might be the most suitable units for me. He made the point that with my School Certificate, I would have more chance of promotion in a unit which was always looking out for men with more education, and suggested the Royal Corps of Signals. This 'clicked' with me because I already had basic signalling qualifications and some experience. So I signed up – for eight years regular service, plus four years in the Army Reserve. In those days that was usual, quite different from 60 years later. There were only four ways to get out: by being 'bought out'; 'discharged as physically unfit for any form of military service'; 'dismissed in disgrace'; and 'discharged dead'.

So off I went to Catterick Camp in North Yorkshire, to the Depot Battalion of the Royal Corps of Signals, as '2323839'. It was winter, and all the squads were housed in oblong huts, with a coal stove in the middle, and a cubicle at one end for the NCO [non–commissioned officer] in command of the squad. It was a matter of chance whether one got a decent NCO or not – but one soon found that there was a sort of rule about this: the more senior the better. Ours was at the very bottom end — a 'lance corporal, acting, unpaid' — and he was a nasty bit of work. Needless to say, he had little time for recruits with education, and I might have had a very rough time. What saved me was my previous military experience and training (though I had enough sense not to tell him about it). I just found it easier than most of the other raw recruits to deal with drill and uniform etc.

The large tarmac area where all the squads learned their drill was known as 'the square' — and it was not quite on the level. One of his tricks was to march us down the slope, and then make us go up it 'at the double'. One day, somebody stumbled and fell: the lance–corporal immediately turned the whole squad around to double back over the poor chap, before he could get up. In due course, we were fitted for our uniforms by the Depot tailor. The tunic was right up to the neck, and with brass buttons. When you tried one on that was nearly the right size for you, the tailor said 'Breathe out!', before he measured the chest, so that when you breathed normally the tunic would fit very tightly. In those mid–1930s the Signals were still nominally a mounted corps, so we wore 'wing' breeches, puttees and spurs. The breeches were as nearly skin–tight as he could get them: it was difficult to put them on quickly until they had stretched from being worn, and it was quite common for us to pull them off for one another.

There was an offence known as 'dumb insolence' – not difficult to achieve when one said nothing in response to an eyeball–to–eyeball glare – and the bellowed question [for example] 'What the hell do you think you're doing?'. Our lance–corporal (acting unpaid) liked to take a firm grip of a man's tunic between two buttons, and rock him back and forth on his feet — which were of course close together 'at attention', with arms straight down, hands behind the outer seam of one's breeches. When without warning he let go, the man had to try not to fall down backwards. Not all succeeded.

Alastair—second from left

Most of our off–duty time during the week was taken up by all the 'spit–and–polish' needed on our uniforms. So far as leather items were concerned, that expression was literal: boots; chinstrap across the front of the cap; and the bandolier (worn diagonally across the chest) with its array of pouches and flaps. For kit inspection, the soles (and iron studs thereon) of one's spare boots had to be polished. It's not worth listing all the rest of what was called 'bull' (except to say that in our Depot we did *not* paint the coal).

Predictably, I was selected for the rifle team. This led to an amusing episode. One Sunday morning, a few of us were sitting on our beds polishing equipment, reading or just talking, when a couple of sergeants came in. We all leapt to our feet and stood to attention, but one of them said 'Easy – carry on'. Then 'Is one of you called Heron?', at which I stood up again and answered 'Sergeant'. They nodded, and told me to come along with them. We went to the arms store, which they unlocked, and once inside one of them said 'Is it true you're quite a good shot?', to which I replied that I could manage quite well. 'Right — choose yourself a rifle.' These were standard Service Lee–Enfield .303s, with 'tubes' to take .22–inch ammunition for target practice. By this time I was completely mystified, so when one sergeant said 'You'll probably only need one round, but we'll take two in case', I had a hard job keeping quiet.

The door securely locked behind us, off we went again — to the *tennis court!* And there inside was a very big hare or buck–rabbit, obviously my target. So I hit him behind the base of an ear, he went straight up in the air about a couple of feet, and that was that. They went in and picked him up, we returned to the arms store, where I cleaned the rifle and put it back in the rack. After locking up again, they thanked me and headed for the Sergeants Mess, where no doubt the cook was briefed for a special job.

My reward for this took the form of being asked through the appropriate channel whether I would like assignment to the Sergeants Mess for my 'fatigue' duties. I jumped at it, for probably obvious reasons, and soon added the polishing of glass tumblers to my personal skills. This is as good a place as any to mention that in late 1934 the British Army was so underfunded that it seemed unable to feed its men properly. Relative to the physical demands on us in a severe winter, we never had enough to eat. Our pay was 14 shillings a week, from which 4 shillings were held back. As fortunately I did not smoke, I could spend sixpence in the NAAFI every evening, on a small packet of biscuits to accompany a cup of tea. Three of us got sufficiently desperate one Sunday to 'nick' a loaf from the kitchen stores, which we divided between us and ate just as it was. It's the only thing I've ever stolen in my life: my share may have 'lain on my stomach', but it didn't lie on my conscience.

At the beginning of 1934 (while still in Montreal) I had applied for a short–service commission in the Royal Air Force. The application was acknowledged, but I heard nothing further, and by the time I arrived in London had probably ceased to think about it. Up in Catterick at the Royal Signals I got a surprise. One morning our squad instructor told me that I was ordered to report to the Commanding Officer's parade. He didn't know the reason, but of course off I went. The drill was very formal: the RSM bawled out your name, and you leapt off the bench, stood to attention, and responded 'Sir!'. Then came 'Cap off!', followed by 'March!' (into the CO's office), and 'Halt!'. The CO said 'At ease, Heron', and then asked me when I had applied for a commission in the RAF. I told him, whereupon he said that I was called to appear in London before a selection board. I would be given two days leave, and a rail travel warrant. On my saying 'Thank you, sir', to my surprise the CO smiled slightly and said – to my astonishment 'Good luck, Heron'.

So off I went to London, spent the night with my parents in Brixton, and next morning set out for the Air Ministry in Kingsway. As I was not yet eligible to wear civilian clothes, I had to turn up in full 'undress' uniform, which nevertheless included *spurs*. I was conducted to a narrow corridor, with doors on one side, and benches on the other. There I found myself with the other candidates, all dressed in their best civilian suits, of course! (I didn't realise it at the time, but they were probably all from public schools). In due course, I was ushered into a room, but had to stop immediately I entered the door, because I was facing a long table, covered with green baize cloth, that stretched across the room in front of me. Behind it sat a row of senior RAF officers, plentifully supplied with gold braid etc.. They were plainly astonished, looking at one another questioningly, and then the chairman asked me 'What uniform are you wearing, Heron?', to which I replied 'Royal Corps of Signals, Regular Army, sir'. 'And when did you enlist in the Army?': 'Last December, sir: I had assumed that this application had been unsuccessful'.

The Board then went through my papers, and I was asked a few questions, before being told to wait outside in the corridor. In due course, I was called back, when the chairman of the Selection Board said 'We are agreed that there is no room in the commissioned service of the Royal Air Force for a ranker from the Army. You may go'. So back to Catterick I went, and the next morning presented myself on the CO's parade to report. This I did by quoting the exact words with which I had been dismissed in London. The CO looked at me, smiled, and then said 'In that case, Heron, the Royal Signals will be glad to keep you'. There's a postscript: some time later, one of the sergeants who had heard about the episode said to me 'I hear the CO was very friendly, and you might like to know the reason: he rose from the ranks himself!'

The end of one career

We were getting very near to the end of our 20 weeks' training, and to the passing–out parade of all the squads in that intake. Everybody in our squad was sure that I would be awarded 'the Commanding Officer's whip' as the best recruit in our squad — no great achievement, considering the head start I had over all the other men. I woke up during the night shivering, and at 'Reveille' found myself so weak and ill that I told them to let the lance–corporal know that I'd have to 'report sick'. He had the sense to know that was the last thing I wanted to do, and was probably the last man in the squad to try to 'pull a fast one', so he agreed. I had to get dressed and out to the edge of the square, and wait until the sick parade was told to form up. When it did, I was the most senior recruit, so I had to 'march us off' to the Medical Hut.

When the RAMC doctor had finished examining me, he said 'I'm sending you into hospital'. I begged him not to do so, as I was just about to pass out, but he was adamant. So in a different sense I 'passed out' while in the ambulance.

When I regained consciousness I was in bed with an oxygen mask on my face, and my father sitting beside the bed. I had pericarditis — inflammation of one of the linings of the heart — and I had nearly 'not made it'. So I never passed out, and the man in my squad who got my CO's whip brought it in to get my hands on it for a few minutes. Three months in Catterick Military Hospital was a revelation. The RAMC major in charge of my case was very pleasant and friendly, but the same could not be said of the senior nursing staff. Most of the actual bedside nursing was carried out by male RAMC medical orderlies; they worked under the direction of the nursing sisters, members of the Queen Alexandra's Imperial Military Nursing Service — the QAs for short. Obviously their personalities varied, and some were friendlier than others, but our ward's 'Queen bee' was a rigid disciplinarian martinet. When eventually it was decided by the doctors that I could get up and walk about, she gave orders that I was to make my bed, 'like everyone else'. I did not dare to tell the RAMC doctor: she would have made my life in the ward even harder.

After four months in hospital, the final decision was to discharge me from the Army on medical grounds. I was bitterly disappointed, because despite all the hardships of the training period, I had grown to feel that I would do well in the Signals. It was my friend Peter Sale, who won the CO's whip in the next squad behind ours, who did, rising to the rank of RQMS from training as an instrument mechanic, and being mentioned in despatches by Montgomery in the Western Desert. After that, he was shipped back to Britain, and following a period of technical duty based at Weymouth, took his discharge in early 1946, after nearly 12 years service. So Peter joined Bob and Sam to form my trio of nearly–lifelong close friends – as different from one another and from me as one could imagine.

Back to 'Civvy Street'

By the time that I came to the end of my time in hospital, and returned to civilian life, my parents were living in a semi–detached house in a Surrey suburb of Greater London, called Worcester Park. That certainly implied that my father had got quite a decent job, though I can't remember its nature. But my new life of unemployment did not last long: in spite of taking things quietly, I found myself back in hospital. This was called the Princess Beatrice Hospital, in Earls Court in west London – like all pre–NHS institutions supported by voluntary contributions. The senior doctors and surgeons all held 'Honorary' appointments, and gave their services to the hospital and its patients without charge. There were few 'domestic staff', and probationer nurses did most of that work as well as what they were there for. The wards of course were 'Nightingale': mine was about the length of a cricket pitch, with two rows of beds facing each other, a table at the entrance end for the staff nurse on ward duty, and what were called the 'sluices' at the other end (the place where bedpans etc were washed and sterilised, plus toilets for those patients able to walk about). The windows there, as I discovered when eventually I was ambulant, looked out on a cemetery. So far as I know, there was no direct route there from the hospital mortuary, but it was a bit macabre.

I came under the care of a 'heart specialist' (=consultant cardiologist today) who 'had his rooms' in Wimpole Street (next to the better–known Harley Street). When he took my case history, and I came to the point where mention was made of the 'make your own bed' regime, he said sternly 'Mr Heron, you must not make allegations like that!' to which I replied quietly 'But that is what happened, sir'. He was clearly shocked, as well he might be, and I often wondered if he ever took the matter up officially, or through medical colleagues in the RAMC. In those days, quite the opposite of present practice, the regime for heart conditions was 'total rest': when Sister saw me reading my only book, the Complete Works of Shakespeare, she practically snatched it out of my hands because 'it was far too heavy'! She ordered a book–rest, and my book was restored. Incidentally, I read right through all the plays and the Sonnets, to my enduring profit in later life.

We had one main meal a day, but patients who liked 'an egg to their tea' were wholly dependent on their relatives or visitors. As I had no visitors, I didn't get any eggs – but I gradually built up an understanding with the nurses that I could eat as many slices of 'bread and scrape' as they were prepared to give me: by the time I could help with serving out the teas, I'd got my 'normal' ration up to fifteen slices (they were thin). I never established why neither my mother nor my father managed to visit me there, after a couple of times in my first fortnight, but it was possibly the cost of the return journey by train and bus from Worcester Park.

When I was discharged after three–and–a–half months, I was given an appointment to see my doctor in Wimpole Street. He showed me the very simple electro–cardiograph that he had obtained. In those days, this was a tracing made by a stylus on the smoked paper fitted round a revolving drum. On the basis of his clinical examination and the ECG evidence, he told me that I had made a remarkable recovery, and that if I followed the instructions he was about to give me, I could eventually look forward to a completely normal life. And the instructions? Not to run a single step for twelve months, whatever the circumstances. 'Get used to walking up and down stairs – even when the telephone or door bell is ringing; get used to watching the bus pull away that you could have caught by running for it and so on: do you think you can discipline yourself as much as that for a year?' 'Yes, sir' I replied.

When I saw him again a year later, he was well–satisfied with the ECG and his examination, and said 'Did you really manage not to run?' I nodded. 'Well now, just carry on sensibly, very gradually increasing the amount of exertion; run a few steps and gradually increase the amount as you feel no ill–effects. Eventually you will feel able to take more vigorous exercise, probably even to play tennis, for example'. He shook hands and said that he did not expect that I would need to see him again, The contrast between his 1935 approach to treatment and that of sixty years later could hardly be more striking, yet he was absolutely right, and in physical terms I was able to live a perfectly normal life. I have always been grateful to him.

Starting again

By then I was just turned 20. My mother and father decided that it would be better if they lived separately, so she and I, with her elderly aunt, went to live in a small terraced house on a new estate just outside Dartford, in Kent; my father went into lodgings in south London. To make a fresh start, I signed as an articled clerk with an accountant, who had his small office near Finsbury Square at the north end of Moorgate in the City of London. Most of his clients were small businesses in north–east London. He had one fairly experienced clerk and a typist. Very soon I was thrown in at the deep end, first working with the other clerk out at clients, and then left to myself while he went to other clients. I could not have asked for a better opportunity, far better than I would have got in a large firm of accountants. Here I should explain that it was customary to pay a premium for one's articles, which went up with the status of the firm. As we could not afford anything at all, my employer not only took me on without a premium, but even gave me £1 a week towards my rail season–ticket.

Once a week I went with another articled clerk from a different office for a session with a tutor appointed by the Association of Incorporated Accountants (then second in size and status to the Institute of Chartered Accountants). I was enrolled in a correspondence course with the Metropolitan College in St Albans; this was excellent, and required a weekly piece of homework, based on the prescribed reading and practice, which was returned the next week with critical comment and advice. The course prepared students, entirely by correspondence, for the Intermediate and Final examinations, Success depended upon a combination of aptitude and sustained self–discipline. I soon found, both at work and in my studies, that I was fortunate in having the aptitude — I actually enjoyed dealing with all the figures — and all my life up to then had prepared me for the self–discipline. It was just as well.

On my own

In October 1936, having at the age of 51 not quite escaped from a menopausal depression, my mother committed suicide. Apparently she and her aunt had 'crossed swords' again, and mother left the house with our Old English sheepdog, crossed the fields to the main railway line, and lay down across the rail. Her funeral took place on my 21st birthday. My father and I met at the inquest and at the funeral, then again two or three times during the next month. This gave him a chance, which he took, to recognise that I was now a man, and we drew together for the first time. Shortly after, he went into hospital for a minor operation (hernia), and as was not uncommon succumbed to post–operation pneumonia. I sat on one side of his bed, facing the nursing nun across the bed for some hours (it was a Roman Catholic voluntary hospital). Eventually, she caught my eye, glanced at the oxygen mask on my father's face, and looked back at me. I nodded affirmatively, and she removed it: he slipped away peacefully soon after. So I arranged another funeral, and then — the task of helping my very frail great–aunt to re–settle, in a London nursing home.

There are in London two congregations of the Church of Scotland, as distinct from the Presbyterian Church in England: Crown Court Church, Covent Garden, and Pont Street in Mayfair. I had for some time been attending the latter, and recently come into membership taking my 'first communion'. I had also made the acquaintance of some other young men on Sunday mornings, and at social events. One evening, four of us went for dinner nearby, and ended up in the 'bedsit' of one of them. Discussion on matters of personal religious belief brought out the fact that two of them were active in a movement then known as the 'Oxford Group'. I accepted an invitation to meet with others of their number, mainly because I was impressed by the quiet depth of conviction and what I could only call a 'caring attitude' that they showed.

The Group was an evangelical movement, in the strict sense of having 'good news' to share with others, not in the theological sense of salvation doctrine with which most people associate the term. As a movement, it was fully ecumenical within a Christian context, placing emphasis upon the accessibility of the Holy Spirit to each one, and in the affairs of everyday life. The movement had a strong ethical emphasis, expressed through its four 'absolute standards', of honesty, love, purity and unselfishness. The aim of 'life–changing' was much to the fore, and I would be both ungrateful and less than honest if I failed to record that my own life was radically changed through my encounter with the original Oxford Group. I had never read or heard of the Quaker movement, but unwittingly I was passing through the experience Quakers traditionally called 'convincement': the deep inward realisation, the conviction, of self–centredness and self–will that alienates the soul from God. And I began the life–long process of 'conversion', of freely–chosen open–ness to 'being changed' inwardly. It was no sudden 'Damascus road' event for me, but the beginning of an adventure of the spirit, a journey into the unknown.

2 Encounters

Soon after starting work in the City of London ('the Square Mile'), my daily commuting by train from Dartford to London Bridge provided the opportunity for my first 'falling in love'. Betty worked in a music shop quite close to my office, so we not only travelled together on the train, but often walked across London Bridge, past the Bank of England, and up Moorgate (or in reverse). We went several times to the Henry Wood Proms at the Queen's Hall (opposite the BBC, later destroyed in the Blitz), and to the then very popular big dance spots. On my birthday, after Mother's funeral, Betty took me off for a long country walk in Kent, ending up in a quiet tiny pub with a big log fire. She had known personal loss and grief, her fiancé having been killed in a motor–cycle crash. Given my economic situation, there was no question of us becoming officially engaged, but we felt like that about things. So she had me down to stay with her and her parents at Christmas, when I gave her an unofficial betrothal gift – a wristwatch. On New Year's Eve we went up to the Streatham Palais for dancing (with several hundred others.), and 'saw the New Year in'. I took the opportunity of introducing her to my Aunt Molly, who lived in Streatham: she approved!

Things went on normally until one evening in late February, when as usual I picked her up as she left work, and we started walking to London Bridge. After a minute or two, Betty told me that she had accepted a marriage proposal from the manager at her work; that she was very sorry because she realised I would be severely hurt; but that she hoped I would understand her difficulty in facing a very long wait before I would be qualified and in a proper job, enabling us to get married.

I was completely crushed, even though I did see her problem, and made my way home to my digs. It was the only time in my life when I felt suicidal, but common sense prevailed, and later I came to see that she had been right.

Facing the facts

When I came to clear up my parents' affairs, I soon found that almost all the furniture in the house was on hire–purchase. Most of it was re–possessed to

clear the account, and I watched it go (remembering the bailiffs in Montreal.).
I made a vow to myself that for the rest of my life I would 'buy my necessities
for cash: only "luxuries" could be on hire–purchase'. Then I went looking for
a bed–sitting room as close to my work in the City as possible: This turned
out to be a semi–basement room with a family in Stoke Newington, which
'took me to its heart'. Obviously I could not live on £1 per week, even with
the small subsidy from my great–aunt, so I had no alternative but to obtain
release from my articles, and seek a job as an unarticled clerk. I applied for
several, but because of my limited experience was lucky to get even one
interview. This was with a firm near Baker Street, in Gloucester Place, with a
very different clientele from that of my previous firm. The man who
interviewed me said 'We will let you know our decision' – but in fact called
me in for a second interview, when he asked me several of the same questions
again. Eventually he said 'Do you really think that you can meet the demands
of this post?', to which I replied confidently 'Yes, sir – I'm sure that I can'. So
I got the job (at two pounds ten shillings a week).

My great–aunt died of cancer some months later, leaving her small 'estate' to
me as her only relative. As she had also made me her executor, I had not only
to arrange her funeral, but obtain probate of the will – good practice for a
young would–be professional. At work, not only did I enjoy the more
demanding complicated accounting and auditing, but began going to student
meetings at the headquarters of the Incorporated Accountants. Being
unarticled, I faced a period of four more years before I would be allowed to sit
the final examinations. One day the Secretary phoned me at work, and asked
me to come and see him. Mystified, I obtained permission from my chief,
and went along. He explained that a large firm of accountants in Southampton
had enlisted his aid in finding a suitable clerk to fill a post as a 'semi–senior'.
Knowing of my activities in the student society meetings, where I had it
seems acquired a reputation for having come to grips with my subject, and
also about the circumstances in which I had obtained release from my articles,
he wondered if I might be interested. I went back to my chief (the same man
who had interviewed me twice) and asked for his advice, making it clear that
I was very happy with my job, and not wanting to grab the first thing that
turned up. He told me to let them arrange for me to be interviewed, and then
to come back to him with the outcome. This I did, having been offered the

post. Pointing out that in our small firm I might have a long wait for promotion, he thought my prospects would be better in the Southampton firm, though he added 'we will be very sorry to see you go, Heron: you have justified my hopes for you here'.

Away from London

So in the summer of 1938 I cycled the 80 miles to Southampton, to find digs for myself and make arrangements to start my new work. I found the former in a quiet road just behind the then new Polygon Hotel, not far from the Civic Centre buildings. The other lodgers with our widowed landlady were the owner–manager of the chemist's shop in the High Street, and an articled clerk from my own new office. We all got on well together, and I stayed there in Morris Road until I left Southampton on 3 September 1940. By the way: the young clerk was the son of R.J.Mitchell, the designer of the 'Spitfire' fighter aircraft,

The firm of accountants was the largest in Southampton, with a staff of about twenty, including the typists, and consisted of four partners two of whom were father and son. One of the others had been the founder's clerk from the beginning, the other – much younger – had been offered a partnership after many years service. Fortunately for me, I did most of my work under his direction, and found him able, considerate and absolutely straightforward. What little I had to do with the senior partner and his son was pleasant, and never gave rise to difficulty. The same could not be said for the other senior partner, with whom almost every encounter was a sore trial.

I will confine myself to the noteworthy occasion when he called me to his office on a matter unrelated to my work. As was his custom, he kept me standing on the carpet in front of his desk for a few minutes, while going through some files. Then he started 'Heron, we have noticed that you do not wear a hat'. [He always used the 'royal we' when speaking of the firm's affairs.] 'Yes, sir' I replied, 'I have the misfortune to need a rather large hat, which looks rather odd'. 'That is neither here nor there, Heron: we expect all our clerks to wear a hat when visiting the firm's clients, and you must conform to that rule'. Fortunately his telephone rang at that moment, so I found myself watching, through the window behind him, the beautiful all–white Canadian

Pacific flagship *Empress of Britain* being eased alongside her berth. It gave me the chance to realise that this was not for me a matter of principle, and so discretion was the better part of valour. His call finished, he looked up and said 'Well, Heron?'. 'I would much prefer not, sir, but if you insist .'. 'We do, Heron'. He lowered his gaze to his papers, which was his method of dismissal, except when a conversation had ended with an intention of action of which he approved, when he would always say 'So do'.

The next day I bought a snap–brim felt hat (costing me a quarter of a week's salary), which spent almost all its life on the headlamp of my bicycle. When arriving outside the offices of a client, I would park the cycle against the usual railings, and put the hat on to enter the building, of course removing it as a matter of ordinary courtesy once inside.

I enjoyed the range of my accounting and auditing work, and soon was taking things right up to the final stage, ready for laying before the partner involved. By the end of my first year I had begun to realise that in limited companies the key figure was the company secretary, so decided to aim for the Intermediate examination of the Chartered Institute of Secretaries, instead of that of the Incorporated Accountants. As will be noted later, I passed that examination in June 1940, fully intending to take the Final whenever the war came to an end. But whatever might be the direction I took, my professional training, together with a varied practical experience, would be a worthwhile asset.

A new family

When I moved to Southampton from London in 1938, I was provided with the names and addresses of people there who were active in the Oxford Group, and encouraged to make myself known to them. This I did, and so came to be welcomed by Ethel and Will Metherell, the former being one of the two daughters and four sons of a well–known Southampton builder and property developer, the latter a retired builder with a Devon family background. They in turn had four daughters, one married and living near Chichester; one an Octavia Hill–trained house property manager, with a job in Newcastle–under–Lyme in the Potteries; and one (the youngest) living at home. I met all three of these during the latter part of 1938, and just before Christmas the fourth daughter, who had been staying with her elder sister and husband, arrived to settle in Southampton with her parents. Their names, in the order just listed, were Elaine, Janet, Elizabeth and Margaret. I was told by Will and Ethel that Margaret had been through what they described as 'a severe nervous breakdown', but was now very much better.

I also met other supporters of the Oxford Group, including several men and women of my own age–group, including Tom Ashton, the newly–appointed curate of a suburban Anglican church. He soon started a youth group, in which many of us became active (including Margaret Metherell) which by the late spring of 1939 was flourishing. The club felt it right to buy and operate a club vehicle on a cooperative pay–as–you–go basis: there was a purse in the glove locker  of the small saloon car into which the users put their agreed 'mileage money', and from which the four drivers drew the cost of petrol and oil, etc.. Looking back, it was remarkable how this simple scheme ran so smoothly, and made possible participation in country outings, and out–of–town meetings for those in our church club with very low incomes.

It soon became obvious that I had been given a new mother and father: Will and Ethel simply made me 'one of the family'. This process was furthered by the simple friendliness – eventually friendship – of their resident housekeeper/cook Nora. Fairly described as 'buxom', certainly as 'comfortable', she was not only a superb cook, but a superb listener. With our generation she knew how to be firm, and could 'steady' one when things were proving difficult. Because of Margaret's long psychiatric illness, Nora was rightly a bit protective of her, and naturally interested in whether a new male friend was likely to contribute to continued recovery, or otherwise.

Early in 1939, Margaret decided to become a nurse, and entered the Southampton Children's Hospital as a probationer. She already had a BSc in horticulture, from the University of Reading, so the academic side would not

Will and Ethel Metherell (Margaret's father and mother) (1940) ... they made me 'one of the family'

pose any fresh problems. Although the frequent inability to provide effective treatment (in those pre–antibiotic days) often led to sad outcomes, she enjoyed the practical side, despite the fact that in 1939 student nurses still did most of the domestic work on the wards. Off duty, she was very active in our church youth club, and increasingly chose to spend time with me when her off–duty and my free time coincided. The latter was very limited, because I had to work at least 15 hours a week on my correspondence course, and be certain to get my scheduled homework posted every week without fail. If I took an evening off, I had to make it up at the weekend.

We also joined with Will and Ethel in local and sometimes national activities of the Oxford Group, as did Margaret's next younger sister Janet (up in the Potteries). Looking back, I realise how immature I was for my age, despite my success in coping with difficulties and family disaster. My need for a continuing process of inward spiritual change was all too obvious: the saving feature was that I knew it, and accepted that an attitude of lifelong willingness was being asked of me. I had just enough insight to realise that I must put my trust in the love of God, not in my own capacity for change.

The way of non-violence

By the time war was declared at the beginning of September 1939, I had worked through the problem of what this particular ex–soldier had to face. In the simplest terms, I was unable to imagine Jesus of Nazareth killing anyone, for whatever reason. As a willing disciple neither could I do so. My situation was made much less difficult by the fact that Will, Ethel and Margaret were supportive – and by the fact that I could discuss the problem with my own age–peers in the church club, even though all but a few did not share my position. But opposition came from two of the full–time workers for the Group, known well to us in Southampton, and certainly as close mutual friends. They were very disappointed when they failed to dissuade me from my conviction that I must register as a conscientious objector when the time came. This attitude almost certainly stemmed from the anxiety among leaders of the Group in Britain for it to be perceived as 'patriotic'. Just before the war, in parallel with the post–Munich hasty programme of national re–armament, a decision was taken to change the name of the Group to 'Moral Re–armament.'

Most of my colleagues at the office were remarkably understanding; my landlady and the two men in my digs found it pretty difficult, but we achieved mutual respect and carried on as friends, once they had understood my situation. In due course I registered as a conscientious objector, and ended my statement by offering to serve in the Medical Corps: of that more later.

In mid–September 1939, Margaret and I decided to snatch a short holiday, after I had phoned a couple near Middlesbrough who said they would be glad to put us up for a night on arrival, and again when we were leaving; they could also direct us to a favourite camping spot in the North Yorkshire Moors, inland from Whitby. The couple in question were Ruth and Norman Gaudie, Quakers to whom I had been referred for advice in 1938 when I was trying to help a man I had met when attending services at the Methodist Central Hall in Aldwych, under Donald Soper.

Norman Gaudie [top right], Ruth Gaudie [bottom left], Martyn Gaudie [bottom right].
(c. 1938)

They were the first Quakers I had met, and later became life–long personal friends.

One of our youth club offered the loan of a tent and flysheet (with the advice to minimise possible criticism by using the flysheet as a second tent!), and with other family and borrowed equipment we set off to the North. It was an epic trip in some ways, including the refusal of the car to start when at the bottom of the hill where we camped by the little stream in Hob Hole; a visit to Captain Cook's birthplace at Staithes, where the fishermen's wives called the policeman because they thought we might be German spies; and my lumbar spine going into painful spasm that made getting in and out of the car on the return journey south a bit of a nightmare. The first time, Margaret thought it was very funny, which certainly placed a strain upon our now closer relationship. [Yes: we did use the flysheet as a second tent, and both got home still virginal!]

An 'engagment' photo taken in Bristol (1940)

Commitment

In February 1940, I asked Will and Ethel how they felt about Margaret and I getting engaged. They then explained in detail about the circumstances and the course of her 'nervous breakdown', and the possibility of a recurrence at some time. If she and I felt it right to go ahead, believing it was God's loving purpose for us, we had their blessing and full support. We went together to choose a simple ring [a small sapphire between two diamonds], and one evening went down to the little Saxon–Norman church in South Stoneham where we all usually worshipped, and 'plighted our troth'.

In June we went to Bristol, and stayed with a widowed lady friend of one of Marg's former nurses during her illness, while each day for five days I sat the examinations for my 'Inter' of the Chartered Institute of Secretaries. The weather was fine – and hot – so it was all done in shirtsleeves. One afternoon, things having until then been going well, I walked into the kitchen where Marg was with our hostess getting tea, and said to Marg 'How do you feel about marrying a dustman?', to which she replied 'It wouldn't make any difference. Why?'. 'This afternoon's paper was on Mercantile Law', I replied, 'and I wrote everything relevant that I knew, on all five questions, in 25 minutes. I spent the next two and a half hours trying to think of anything to add – without success'. Well, a tired examiner must have been so pleased not to be faced by a lot of waffle, that he gave me a pass! Later on, I had a letter from the secretary to the examining board to say that I had obtained the overall highest marks at that centre for the week's work.

Becoming a 'CO'

Shortly after our return I appeared before the local tribunal for conscientious objectors. There was a chairman and two assessors, assisted by the Clerk of the tribunal. My statement was read out, then the supporting letters from my referees. After a short consultation with his colleagues, the Chairman said that they were satisfied of my sincerity, and were prepared to register me as a conscientious objector. There was however a problem: the tribunal had just been informed that 'there were no vacancies at present in the Royal Army Medical Corps', the service which I had put forward as the 'condition' for my registration. In the circumstances of the war, this was bizarre, but the Chairman then said 'What else are you willing to offer as conditional service, Mr Heron?'.

Everybody then had to wait while I sought an answer to that unexpected question. I remembered the New Testament words 'You will know in that moment what you must say', and was 'still' inwardly. Then I asked 'What about the civilian ambulance services?'. They whispered together and then the Chairman said 'Yes; your registration is conditional upon you enrolling in the ambulance service within two weeks from today'. That was that.

Baptism of fire

I had already given in my notice to the firm, and I was soon a driver in the Southampton Ambulance Service. As the Battle of Britain commenced in the air, Southampton had its first bombing raid, in mid–afternoon, by low–flying fighter–bombers that aimed at the port. Some bombs fell on buildings at the bottom of the main street (Below Bar) leading to the pier and the dock area. Within minutes I had my first experience of finding a casualty – dead from blast inside a shattered building. When I slid my hand underneath the body to share with my mate the lift onto a stretcher, I realised that I was feeling the exposed spine – and reflexly snatched my hand back, Then the thought came very clearly to me: 'He's not there any more – go ahead'. So we did – and then carried on searching the ruins for other casualties. In between raids, we assisted with ordinary ambulance duties around the city alongside the regular staff (who were of course automatically exempt from military service).

In mid–August, the station officer greeted me one morning with 'Hello Heron! the boss wants to see you at the Civic Centre at 1030 today, so take a car.' In reply to my puzzled question, he simply said he had no idea what I was wanted for. ('The boss' was the Medical Officer of Health for the city). So off I went, was greeted by the MOH's secretary, and shown into his room. He greeted me warmly and asked me to take a seat, but then seemed at a loss to know how to start the conversation. Eventually he said as much, and went on to tell me that the City Council had passed a resolution, dismissing all conscientious objectors from the City's payroll. It hadn't occurred to anybody that there might be one in the Ambulance Service – so he was faced with 'the miserable task' (his words) of giving me a fortnight's notice, adding that it was made worse by the good report he had received of my conduct during and after the first bombing raid. He wished me well and shook me warmly by the hand, and showed me out himself instead of calling his secretary. He also said that he would provide me with a testimonial that I could use when seeking a fresh post. When I got back to our station, many of the chaps said how sorry they were about this enforced end to my service with them.

As things turned out, the last day of my two weeks notice coincided with the first night of what came to be known as 'the Blitz' on London. I picked Marg up as she came off duty at the hospital, and we went home to consider my next action with Will and Ethel. Sitting down together in silence, in what the Group called a 'Quiet Time', we sought God's guidance for me. When I shared my sense that I should go up to London in the morning, to seek an opportunity for service there, they all felt this to be right. As our church youth club could no longer make use of the communal car, I had become responsible for it as owner, and so could use it freely.

London in the Blitz

So the next morning, I set off for London. As I came nearer to the centre, around County Hall and Waterloo Station, I was frequently diverted by closed streets and could see more and more bombed buildings, some still smoking from the fires started by the incendiary bombs. I managed to get near to County Hall, where I knew I would find the headquarters of the London County Council Ambulance Service, and managed with the aid of my letter from Southampton to gain admission to the office of the hard–pressed and weary Director. He read the letter, asked me a few questions, and then said something like 'Of course I'd like to take you on, especially now, but I can't: the LCC won't employ COs either'. I was of course amazed and dismayed, and simply asked him for advice. He then suggested that I try to get into the Light Rescue Service in one of the London boroughs.

The nearest to the City of London was Islington, so I set off to its Town Hall in Upper Street. Soon I was in the office of its MOH, presenting my letter, and mentioning that I had just driven up from Southampton, pausing only at County Hall. He seemed to be 'sizing me up', and then said 'I am willing to take you on – but I've no idea what kind of reception you'll get at the depot: they are a pretty hard lot of customers'. On my saying that I was fully prepared to 'have a go' on that basis, he phoned the depot superintendent and explained the position. Apparently he also said that he was 'willing to have a go' with me – so after filling in the necessary paperwork I set off to the depot, located in the buildings of the China Inland Mission at Islington Green.

I parked the car some distance away, and just walked in and asked for the office. The superintendent (previously a public health inspector in the borough) explained the shift system (24 hours on, 24 off), said he was particularly glad to have another driver, and took me over to a room with six beds (very basic!). We agreed that I would go straight off to seek some nearby bed–and–breakfast accommodation, and report for duty the next morning. So I was the first CO in the Islington Rescue Service: when I left three and a half years later, there were thirteen. I suppose that I had been a sort of 'guinea pig'.

Soon after my start in Islington, one of Marg's maternal uncles and his wife invited me to tea at their home in Hampstead. Knowing that he managed the family properties in north London, I asked him whether I might be able to rent a one–bedroom flat, and fend for myself instead of in bed–and–breakfast, plus evening meals 'out' when I was off duty. He said he would look into it, and let me know, suggesting that I phone him in a week's time. When I did, he was able to tell me that there was in fact a small flat empty in Muswell Hill that might be suitable. But he then went on immediately to ask 'Are you and Margaret thinking of getting married?'. To this I could only reply 'No', of course – at that moment.

It had become completely natural for me to seek God's guidance – and I had plenty of opportunity to sit or walk in silence, seeking only to be open. Gradually it became clear to me, not only that I should ask Marg how she felt, but that it would be right to tell her about the flat – and to propose a date for the wedding! So I did this – and she made it very clear on the phone that this was what she felt right too. The 'date' was six weeks ahead: Saturday 16 November, her 28th birthday.

A wartime marriage

The invitations asked people to 'waive the usual formality of gifts' in view of the wartime circumstances. We hoped this would enable some to come even from a distance, using the money for their fares. In the event, there were

Ken Collins and Aunt Molly

about a hundred people at the little church at South Stoneham, on the outskirts of Southampton. I arrived in the small Ford car, bringing from London both my Aunt Molly and the organist – Ken Collins, the assistant organist at Winchester Cathedral prior to his call–up as a CO, and like me in London to work in the Blitz. After the reception at home, we defied convention and the bride and groom drove off back to London with aunt and organist!

Having dropped them off. Marg and I went on to the little flat, on which I had been working when off–duty during the six weeks. As I lifted her over the threshold, the air–raid sirens went off, and so our wedding night was 'normal' for those times.

It didn't take long for Marg to discover that, despite the obvious need, no nurse–teaching hospital in London was prepared to admit her to complete her nursing training – because she was married. So she signed–up as a car driver in the Ambulance Service (taking care to be on the same 24–hour shift as myself.). The London blitz lasted about eight months,

The happy couple!
At South Stoneham Church, Southampton 16.11.40

culminating on the night of 10 May 1941, when the Luftwaffe delivered its heaviest and most sustained attack, I shall always remember stopping our truck on the bridge over Archway Road, and seeing the whole of the City and the East End burning. This is the place to note that the real heroes of the Blitz were the firemen, often battling against impossible odds. In the Rescue Service we were 'at risk' of course, when we went out to an 'incident' during a prolonged raid, and it was always possible that a damaged building would collapse on top of us. But it was pretty routine activity, and one got used to it.

When the raids stopped, time hung heavily in the 24–hour shifts, and there was a sort of reaction to all the months of activity. For me the bottom was reached on the day when I found myself unable to get up from my bed in the drivers' room, in mid–afternoon, without saying out loud 'Now you are going over to the canteen to get a mug of tea'. Fifty years later this very slowly became recognised as one of the typical post–stress reactions. There was an obvious limit to how much time could be filled up by playing snooker, or table tennis, or by reading. During the summer and autumn we had teams playing cricket or football, against teams from other depots; in the evenings mostly table tennis and darts. This included some ambulance service depots, where there were women as well as men: it was an eye–opener for us to be offered refreshments on a table with a table cloth. During the day, most of us were engaged on the demolition of bombed buildings, unskilled work but requiring one to remember not to knock bricks off the wall on which one was sitting!

Weekend university

In September 1941, another CO (Stan Martin, the son of a colliery manager in County Durham)) and I decided that we had to do something constructive with all this idle time. On enquiry, we found that the only college of London University not to be evacuated was Birkbeck College, in the City near Chancery Lane. Traditionally a part–time college, it was operating on Saturday and Sunday, instead of weekday evenings. When we enquired at the office about the possibility of becoming 'occasional students' (since we would have to go alternate Saturdays/Sundays), we were offered a choice between geography and psychology. Stan fully intended to become a Methodist minister, so he opted for psychology. And so did I – for a quite different reason. I remembered hearing Marg's mother saying one day that she wished someone in the family would learn something about psychology. So we signed–on and started going to the lectures. There were also 'practicals': a laboratory class involving (literally) brass instruments.

As by September 1942 there had been no resumption of bombing raids, we asked the Superintendent if permission could be obtained for us to go (on our bicycles about 15 minutes) when on duty. Authority was obtained, so we were able to sign–on as ordinary students, attending every Saturday and Sunday. I enrolled for what was called the 'Academic Diploma in Psychology': strictly speaking, this was supposed to be post–graduate, but the lecturer in charge arranged for it to be taken at an undergraduate level (because of the wartime circumstances). I didn't know it then, but this laid the foundation for a career change. In due course I took the examination, with a first–class pass, and in October 1943 started on a BSc degree course.

Over that winter, having already been active in the Students Union, I was elected President, which carried with it a seat on the Board of Governors , of which the chairman was Archbishop William Temple. Sometime in the Spring of 1944 the College held its Founders Day, and invited Herbert Morrison (the Minister responsible for all the fire, rescue and ambulance services) to give the Oration. It fell to me to second the vote of thanks to him. I started off by saying that, as everyone in the balcony (the student body) would know, I was incapable of just being polite – and then I paused while everybody held their breaths! Then I continued by saying that fortunately I could express sincere appreciation for the address that we had just heard, and to thank the Orator on behalf of the students of the College. There was a roar of applause. Later there was a formal lunch, and I found myself sitting next to Morrison. At some point there was some discussion about anarchism as a philosophy, in the course of which Morrison said that he had known one successful anarchic community. Without pausing to think, I said 'Are you sure, sir?'. He swung round to look straight at me (with his good eye), hesitated, then said 'No' – which I thought did him great credit.

Life in the Rescue Service

There are some incidents that have stayed vividly in my memory. Food rationing during the war was both strict and successful, and although there was a 'black market' it was on a relatively small scale. One day, a couple of the men arrived with a crate of eggs, containing 72 one–dozen boxes. These sold like the proverbial 'hot cakes' on our shift. Late in the afternoon, I was sitting on my bed in the drivers room, reading, when the door opened and five or six men came in, closing the door behind them. Nobody said anything: they just stood there. Quite mystified, I asked 'What's all this in aid of?'. Then one of them asked 'Why didn't you buy any eggs?'. I had to make them wait while I thought about this, and then I said 'because I think rationing is the fair way of dealing with short supplies, but as you all know I don't try to impose my views on other people: it's up to each of us to decide what is right to do in any particular case'. Nobody said anything, and they all filed out, leaving me alone. Then the door burst open, and one of them, a fellow–driver who both owned a pub and played the violin (sometimes on the BBC), said with great emotion 'If you ever let me down, I'll never forgive you!' – and went out. I was very touched and moved by this, but also made conscious of my own fallibility, and how easy it could be to compromise with my beliefs and principles.

One night, I was on my way to the recreation room, and passed the end of the short passage that contained the squad–leaders room. They were having a heated argument about something, and suddenly I heard the voice of my own squad leader shouting 'I'd rather have my bloody conchies than those !xx!xx!x that you've got!'. Encouraging.

Finding a place to worship

As Margaret and I started our life together in November 1940, we found that we had to address the question of our church affiliation afresh. We had by then, by the way, ceased to be involved in the activities of the former Oxford Group (Moral Rearmament). As we had been active with the Anglicans in Southampton, it was natural that we should start attending the parish church in Muswell Hill. Fairly soon we found ourselves ill–at–ease with the prayers and other support for 'the war effort', and decided to try the local Methodist church. We were made very welcome, and valued the sermons and the singing, but did not feel that we had yet come to the 'right place' for us. Remembering some of our conversation with the Gaudies, we wondered about the Quakers and thought we should investigate. So we went down one Sunday morning to the meeting for worship, at Friends House in Euston Road, opposite Euston

Station. Held in what was called 'the Small Meeting House' (to distinguish it from the large space that could accommodate nearly a thousand people), it was well attended probably by over a hundred.

Although the silence–based meeting for worship was strange to us, sitting in silence was not, since we were well used to the daily discipline of the 'quiet time'. We started attending regularly (on alternate Sundays, of course, because of our 24–hours shift system), and fairly quickly found ourselves feeling at home. We were made welcome, either on our own or with others, in the Bloomsbury homes of some of the members, and enjoyed the discussions that took place. The Quaker peace testimony of course accorded with our position as conscientious objectors, and we began to familiarise ourselves with the history of the Quaker movement since the seventeenth century. We also visited other Quaker meetings in the north London area, notable the one at New Barnet. This provided us with a different setting and group of people, and helped to widen our horizons.

By the end of 1941 we had both reached the point of feeling that we should apply for membership of the Religious Society of Friends. This we did at the same time, but separately on an individual basis. So in January 1942 we met with our respective pairs of 'visitors'. My interesting 'get together' took place in a flat in Bloomsbury (with Eustace Gillett and Charles Lindsay), but we invited Margaret's visitors to come to our home in Muswell Hill. As one of them would face a long journey back, with an air raid all too likely, it was arranged that she would stay overnight with us. This meant her sharing a less than full–size double bed with Margaret – who was six months pregnant. There **was** an air raid, and they didn't get much sleep anyway. The 'visitor' later used to say that Margaret was the 'weightiest' Friend she had ever slept with ! We were both welcomed into membership (of Westminster and Longford Monthly Meeting, as it was then) in February 1942.

Beginning a family

In early 1942 maternity plans had to be made, and it was decided that Marg would go to Oxford for the birth. The actual venue was a small maternity unit located in the residence of the principal of Ruskin College, attached to the Radcliffe Infirmary. This was one of many Emergency Maternity Units set up to meet the needs of London. Keith was born on 14 April, and the next day I drove to Oxford in glorious Spring weather to visit mother and son, both of whom 'were doing well'. Although I don't remember doing so, I must have registered Keith's birth as well as buying Marg a couple of prints (and having them framed). The sister in charge of the unit was horrified when I said that our new son

Lightweight 'carrying hammock' for Keith

'looked a bit like a monkey'! He soon changed and became a very good–looking baby and toddler! A week later I fetched them back to the little Muswell Hill flat, where everything was ready for the new member of the family.

Soon afterwards we passed the car over to Tom Ashton, the former curate in Southampton, who had been my best man at our wedding. He had become an RAF chaplain and was therefore not restricted by petrol rationing. So when during the latter part of August, Marg and I went with Keith for a North Yorkshire holiday, it was by train and bus. The Gaudies arranged accommodation for us in Great Ayton, and we made our excursions from there. One of these included a day trip to our September 1939 camping spot. I had made a very lightweight carrying hammock for Keith, so that Marg and I could cover the necessary cross–country miles there and back. On the way back we experienced a freak snow–storm (in August!), but with an improvised hood Keith survived. We got a lift in the back of a van, and arrived at our lodgings, both very tired but triumphant.

Margaret at Hob Hole, N. Yorkshire (1942)

It later seemed to us likely that Joy was conceived that day – a love child if ever there was, though Marg and I had to recognise that our firm intention to provide a sister or brother

Washing very large quantities of 'nappies'.

for Keith was fulfilled rather earlier than we had intended! Joy was born in the Royal Free Hospital in London on 27 May 1943. As things were going to become somewhat tight in the little flat, we decided to buy (from Uncle Will) a house near Finsbury Park that had been repaired after earlier bomb–damage. There was no running hot water supply, so we heated the water for baths in an electric metal boiler in the kitchen, then carried the hot water upstairs in a bucket. Understandably this meant shared baths – Keith and Joy every night, Marg and Alastair once a week! On my off–duty days, I did all the washing, which of course included very large quantities of 'nappies'. I described the array of white flags hanging out on the line as 'unconditional surrender' – but thanks to my mother's way of bringing me up, thought nothing of it. As I recall, my record was forty–two nappies.

Air raids re–started, and one busy night I popped in to see how the family had fared. I was pretty grubby and had a dirty face, and a cheerful Keith (aged 2) pointed this out! Blast from a nearby bomb had blown out the window of his room, and bits of debris were lying on his cot blanket. Marg and Joy were in rooms on the other side of the house, not affected. When news of this incident reached the family, there was pressure for Marg, Keith and Joy to be evacuated from London. So off they went to stay with the Gaudies near Middlesbrough. This coincided with my leaving the Rescue Service (with permission from the authorities dealing with CO affairs) to go into training in Hampstead with the Friends Relief Service, for work overseas when this became possible. By a strange coincidence, I was able to sell the house to an aunt of my Army friend — Peter Sale.

3 Works and faith

At the FRS training centre I was a member of a team being prepared for service in Yugoslavia, but due to the prolongation of negotiations with the War Office its departure was first of all delayed, and then the destination was changed to Greece. Then it was decided that I should be seconded to a small body known as the Inter–governmental Committee for Refugees [IGCR], and sent to Italy with one FRS companion (Dorothea Macdonald). We sailed from Liverpool in February 1945 in the White Star liner *Georgic* (converted as a troopship). To avoid submarine attack, the ship sailed

Family at Mt. Waltham

from north of Ireland right out into mid–Atlantic, then due south until opposite the Straits of Gibraltar, and straight in non stop to Naples. There was one attack, bringing into action one of our escorting corvettes which dropped depth–charges.

Members of FRS team training at Mount Waltham (1944)

Italy in 1945

We found at once how incompetent was the organisation to which we had been seconded: there was no one at Naples expecting us, and no arrangements for us to get to Rome. So I negotiated a lift in the daily courier vehicle, with Dorothea up beside the driver and myself in the back with the mail etc.. On arrival at Rome we were dropped off at the army's Billetting Office, where contact was made by phone with the IGCR office. Later in the day we found ouselves in one of the army's transit hotels, and eventually sitting down to a quite decent Italian meal. Dorothea spoke Italian fluently, having lived there before the war, and she also knew about the food – so my education began with using a fork vertically to deal with spaghetti!

The next day we were picked up by our only colleague (also on secondment, but from the Friends Ambulance Unit) and taken to the office to meet the man in charge. This was a 'Sir' with a double–barrelled name, who did not impress us at all. Here I should explain that fighting was still going on in the North, although the German army was retreating before the combined attack of the British and US forces. As the title implied, the IGCR was supposed to be active on behalf of refugees, of whom there were believed to be many thousands in Italy from various parts of Europe.

In charge on refugee train (1945)

It did not take long to discover that there was no coherent policy or programme, and no financial resources. The director thought in terms of 'projects', and depended for their realisation on the interest and goodwill of the military and Allied Control Commission. Prior to our arrival, he had obtained the use of a sizable villa on the outskirts of Rome, which he wished to serve as a hostel for certain categories of refugees, and he at once put my colleague Dorothea in charge of this project,

For months negotiations had been going on between the authorities in Palestine, the Jewish Agency, the Inter–Governmental Committee on Refugees, the American Joint Distribution Committee, the Allied Commission and Allied Force Headquarters. For weeks selections had been in progress in every part of 'liberated' Italy; for days details had been crystallising out. The Allied Commission and the military authorities were determined that this would be a well–planned 'movement of displaced persons': the relief agencies were equally determined that planning and welfare were not incompatible with Army efficiency. It was at this point that one very newly–arrived Quaker worker got his first assignment: 'You may be able to act as a friendly watcher'.

The movement could be divided into four stages: Assembly, Movement to Centre, The Drill, and Finale.

Assembly:

This took place near Rome, and small groups of people arrived during the course of a week at a refugee camp where they were visited by the representative of the Jewish Agency responsible for the selection, accompanied by members of the Jewish Committees and myself (the 'Friendly Watcher'). Discussions took place with the Camp Commandant and the welfare staff of the camp; the requirements of the Allied Commission's repatriation officer were examined and explained. He had wisely arranged that people should be grouped in parties of twenty–five, using language and nationality as bases, each under a leader selected by the Jewish Committee. The day before the three hundred and fifty from this centre were due to leave for the South, I asked for a meeting of the fourteen group leaders, so that everything could be explained and discussed in detail. German and Italian should have been the languages, and these were used through interpreters for detailed explanation, but essential personal contact was surprisingly well established and maintained with English and French. My role was carefully explained, but some success with welfare problems elevated it from 'friendly watcher' to 'OC Train'!

Movement South:

Three hundred and fifty people with twenty tons of baggage were moved by Army trucks to a nearby remnant of a railway station, where a sixteen–boxcar goods train was loaded, as follows: one car–full of baggage, twenty tons; one car reserved for sick and infirm, with a refugee woman doctor aboard; and fourteen cars with twenty–five people and the rest of their luggage with them in each. One bale of straw had been obtained for each box–car: every person had been *loaned* one Army blanket – and each person in the 'Ambulance Car' lay on a straw–filled palliasse. These scanty amenities plus a first–aid kit, a few hundred cigarettes and some chocolate for the children, were the sort of thing that I could persuade authorities or individuals to lend or contribute. Army rations (prisoner–of war scale) were distributed from the bulk issue by the 'OC Train' (me) and the biscuit tins were then given to the groups as water containers to be refilled at stops, after purity ef supply had been checked.

The journey took thirty–four hours; sanitary arrangements were non–existent, and people took their chance whenever the train seemed to be stopping for some time – a few scrambles occurred, some in the dark, Once a man and a child were left behind, so we waited for them to be brought up by the next train, which at that point was miraculously only half–an–hour behind! Some judicious phoning ahead produced hot water once, for making tea at breakfast. First aid was rendered four times, and two heated squabbles were shamed into silence by a quiet reminder of where they were going, and the need for tolerance and unity in their 'new start'.

It was for this 'friendly watcher' a new experience: diary notes record '…it Is far from easy to be 100% loving towards all these folk I am with …but what sort of a chap would *I* be if I'd been tossed about as they have? …how much the language barrier operates at times of stress; …at other times the actual sharing of their conditions is more than adequate to unite us…'. It was one of the few times such a train–movement had been thus shepherded: these were our minimum standards being applied. These were *people*, though the Army called it a 'movement of displaced persons', and needed to be informed whether the 'bodies' were 'safely delivered'; but it was probably the most comfortable railway trip they had known for many bitter years. It made the 'Friendly Watcher' think pretty hard and deeply.

On arrival at Bari, 'off–loading' commenced, and open five–ton trucks moved first people and then baggage to the transit camp, where those from southern Italy had already assembled. It took seven trucks over four hours to complete this operation, and an incredibly dirty 'OC Train' thankfully ended his mission at 0400. crawled into his sleeping–bag – and slept.

The 'Drill':

The sailing date hed been brought forward, and so the nine hundred had to be passed through 'security', 'medical', 'financial' and 'documents' in just over two days. All the available staff, military and civilian, including now an FAU colleague, plodded on hour after hour. taking meals in relays. Some tempers got a bit frayed, and some decidedly military language was used more than once. I found it very helpful to have the confidence of so many of the people because of our shared experience. My FAU colleague and I worked principally on documentation; some things will be long remembered, especially the red 'J' [Juden] on old German passports, and the shock of comparing people with their photographs seven to ten years old (even though passport photos are seldom flattering). Much patience was shown, and people did try to keep organised, though long waiting and cramped quarters made it difficult. The hardest time was at the very end of the process, when the surplus of candidates over the stipulated nine hundred was at last definitely known: it was only nine – nine unfortunates who could not go. There could be no flexibility: 900 meant precisely that. It would have been easier had the 'surplus' number been greater.

Finale:

The nine hundred made a short overnight rail trip to the port, while we two 'friendly watchers' drove down. I had a few hours sleep on a tiled office–floor, and met the train at 0600 to supervise the last transfer, from station to quayside. Everything went smoothly, and – checked individually by 'Security' for the last time in Italy – they climbed the gangway into the ship.

Yes, the Army knows how to handle a 'movement of displaced persons', but there was room for some 'friendly watching'.

My FAU colleague Sam Marriage went to Palestine with the ship as Liaison Officer – and with only the clothes he stood up in. This was the result of my sheer inexperience, in not realising how essential it was to 'keep an eye' on baggage *all* the time. I should have been sitting with it in the back of the truck on the way down to the port: it was expertly removed, probably by barefooted thieves working in pairs. This was a great blow for Sam, and I felt terrible about it. I had learned a salutary lesson at his expense.

The IGCR Director decided that I should make my base in Bari, but left me to make whatever arrangements I could. Fortunately, Tony Gibson of the Friends Ambulance Unit just then made a similar decision, so we joined forces and presented ourselves to the Town Major – the British Army officer responsible for organising the administration of the city, which included the allocation of office and residential space. He was very friendly and cooperative, and soon identified a large empty house which could serve as both office and residence for the FAU group and myself. We then set to work locating essential furniture, and getting ourselves rationed – entitled to *per capita* allocation of food from an Army depot.

Tony and I then agreed that we should share a secretary, and went back to the Town Major for help, which was readily forthcoming. He started by telling us how he got his own secretary soon after the city was occupied by the British troops. He let his needs be known to the officer in charge of a nearby camp for non–Italian refugees, and then set up a selection session in his headquarters. Having identified the most likely candidate, he asked her how many languages she spoke, to which she replied 'Five, sir'. 'Please list them', he said, which she did: 'French, German, Czech, Serbo–Croat, and Italian'. 'But you have omitted English, in which we are now speaking', he said. 'Oh, yes, sir – I don't count that because I'm not good enough in it'. She got the job, and became a tremendous asset to him.

Well, Tony and I got a secretary, too – a German anti–Nazi refugee from the Bremen area of north–west Germany, who had moved down through Europe from country to country ahead of the German invasions. Intelligent and well–educated, she was also strikingly good–looking. The FAU chaps and I just about managed to 'keep our heads', but when she accompanied me to a concert held in the Opera House, it was almost a royal progress, with every male head swivelling round in admiring envy!

Tony's team were working with Italian displaced civilians and anti–Fascist refugees, which included a large camp down on the north shore of the Bay of Taranto. As my own task – that of locating and counting small clusters of non–Italian refugees – took me through Taranto, I made a short side trip to drop in at the camp. I was made welcome by the FAU member in charge of it, entirely on his own. Having heard him rattling away in Italian to various people, I asked him over our meal how long he had been learning the language, He looked at me, and then burst out laughing: 'I knew only a few words when I was dumped here to cope with this lot (of about 1500 people), so I've picked it up "on the hoof" from sheer necessity.' It was certainly an amazing demonstration in practice of the 'immersion method' of language learning!

On my return journey northwards to Bari, the engine of my not–very–new Army 15cwt truck began to knock, so I stopped at an Army workshop to have it checked. My suspicions of a failing big end in one of the cylinders were confirmed, so I was enjoined to nurse it very slowly all the way to Bari (about 150 miles) and hope it lasted the course. It did, but I reached Bari the day after I had intended, As I approached the city from the south, I saw a large pall of smoke coming up from the port area, and soon learned that I had missed the previous day's disaster: an ammunition ship had blown up in the harbour, resulting in casualties there and in parts of the city itself.

Tony and I both had cause to make brief visits to Rome, so we needed the resources of RAF Transport Command. That required travel orders and we had no superior officer to whom we could turn for these. So we solved the problem quite neatly by signing each other's travel order (not very legibly) and presenting ourselves separately for the same flight. The route from Bari to Naples and Rome crossed the Appenine Mountains, and the RAF pilots frequently flew up the twisting dry–bed river valleys, with a wall of the valley looming up beyond the wing tips on both sides. It was for us a bit hair–raising until we got used to it!

War in Europe ends

But I was on my own, and on the ground, driving through the mountains to Naples, when as I entered the square in the middle of a small town, I heard the news that the war in Europe had ended (12 May 1945). I remember finding it hard to take in, but my feelings of thankfulness soon took over. These were soon followed, as I drove on, by thoughts of all the various needs that would have to be addressed in so many countries. About a fortnight later, when consulting with some American officers in Naples concerned with refugee matters, I

AH with US Army officers and US Red Cross workers, Capri (1945)

heard that a special group was being taken to the island of Capri, in the Bay of Naples. They decided that a Quaker might perhaps be useful, so I was added to the team of American Red Cross and army people going to Capri.

This special group consisted of 72 people found alive in the Dachau concentration camp when it was liberated by the American army. It included the former Chancellor of Austria, Kurt von Schuschnigg, with his wife and daughter; ten Hungarians from the former Horthy regime; eleven people from various countries overrun by the German forces; and forty–eight relatives of those executed for their part in the unsuccessful attempt to assassinate Hitler. This group included the parents, widow and children of Count von Stauffenburg (who led the attempt), and the widow and family of Goerdeler, the Burgermeister of Leipzig. Also released with them were Martin Niemoller, the German Lutheran pastor (and former U–boat commander) who persisted in preaching and writing against the Nazis, whom the Americans accommodated alone in Naples pending the arrival there of his wife and children from Germany.

This unexpected opportunity caused me to write a detailed report to Bertha Bracey, head of the Refugee Section of Friends Relief Service in London, which had seconded me to the Inter–Governmental Committee on Refugees. It is I think worth including here:

'Like most things in life, the present task may be said to have a past, a present and – possibly – a future. With the past. you will already be acquainted: this letter is an attempt to convey some impressions of the present, and of future possibilities that may well have been swept aside or already realised by the time you receive this.

The outstanding feature of the work is the exceptional opportunity it provides to obtain some kind of insight into the popular and personal reaction to the whole idea of 'helping Germans'. It is fair to say that there is widespread fear lest any active Nazis be well–treated, and with this the tendency to identify all Germans as 'part of the machine'. It is perhaps unfortunate that Capri should have been the venue for this small–scale study, as the conditions approach luxury; yet on other grounds this was all to the good for people just released from Dachau and other camps. Several of the group have told me that they realise the unnatural character of this period, but it has been almost a duty to make it plain to many others something of what is facing them in Germany: they find it incredible. The island is being used as an American Air Force rest camp: many of the men have asked me about the group, and in the consequent discussions there has been some evidence of appreciation for a consistent intention to meet need wherever it is found. Many officers have expressed the belief that the 'no fraternisation order' will break down fairly soon, because it originated on a political level remote from the human relations upon which the troops have to work, and several have said that their pay would not last long with the fines they would have to pay for breaches of the order. My impression is that everybody resents any suggestion of pampering, and feel that all assistance should be on a strict subsistence level. Suspicion that many of this group, despite the 'screening', were Nazis until all too recently is fairly general, and this is founded upon the generalisation that any free German MUST have been a Nazi to have remained free so long.

Turning to the group itself, the first impression was of its unity, explained by both Protestants and Catholics as being on a religious basis which has transcended form and dogma, under the stress of a Christian resistance to paganism. This crystallises almost violently in Niemoller's press statement, that his resistance to Hitler was not political but religious. I believe that we shall have to study this very carefully indeed, before we pretend to an understanding of the deep issues involved. Niemoller himself is what is popularly described as 'highly strung', restless and inclined to be aggressive, and I regard it as unfortunate that the inevitable press attacks should have taken place – though the American Forces Headquarters people have held them off very well in the circumstances. He told me that while waiting now to see his wife and children, and to get to grips with things, it was 'worse than the camp in some ways', because a sort of calm – a deep peace at times – had been possible in the routine where 'nothing pended'. I wonder whether it would be possible for someone of unimpeachable integrity in England to invite him to some quiet place where he and his family could be left alone, until he and they find their way through this period? If so, an approach should be made through SHAEF Displaced Persons and the Home Office to ascertain attitudes in view of the bad press he has now had.

Von Schuschnigg is very quiet, and difficult to get much out of; he is probably right in this restraint at present, having regard to the Austrian set–up.

The group has been forthcoming in its recognition of the name Quaker, and people seem appalled that restrictions preventing our work this time are, at least at present, much more severe than for our predecessors.

The fear of 'the fourth Power' (the USSR) is very marked, though it is difficult to assess its origin, as between propaganda and current events. Incidentally, doubt on this score is not confined to them: it is expressed soberly by British and American officers and other ranks.

It would be helpful to have a a fairly clear statement of Friends' policy towards work for Germans and Austrians, both popular – if that is not a misnomer – and unpopular, such as for civilian internees; and in particular, whether I am correct in believing that if it were possible to obtain an entree to project welfare work under Allied Military Government, including such things as re–location, FRS has a concern and the ability to provide workers on request. Despite my efforts to keep in touch with the Society and the Service, my information is now alarmingly out of date. Information Bulletins are not enough.'

I have one rather special memory of my time on Capri. One evening when there was no one around to sit and chat with, I decided to go for a walk down to the beach. Soon I located a path, and some steps, and made my way down. The moon was full, it was of course warm, and there was no one else about. So I stripped off my clothes and swam out in the path of moonlight across the water. I can only describe the experience as magical, unforgettable, unrepeatable. It was also spiritual: I felt a deep sense of being 'part of the scheme of things' – and grateful for it.

For the record, FRS was unable to act upon my suggestions in this report, but made good use of my list of names through the 'search bureau' in its Refugee Section. My idea about the Niemoller family might have been feasible if the Bishop of Chichester had not been out of Britain at the time. Despite his unshakeable pacifist stand, he was held in high regard even in official circles.

In receipt of grace

With the war over, it had become possible for IGCR to move up Italy north of Rome, so it was decided that I be transferred to Rome from Bari, and that I should start gathering information about refugees. I found this work very unsatisfying and depressing, mainly because there were no resources of food, clothing or money with which to relieve the condition of those people I came across. On one of these journeys I found myself at the end of the day billeted for the night in a small house in one of the Umbrian towns. My room was about nine feet square, with white walls. Having set up my camp bed, and got some rations out of my haversack, I sat down on the bed and gazed at the opposite wall. After some time – I have no idea how long – I found myself praying out loud. It was a grumpy prayer, complaining to God about my seemingly useless work in the face of so much need, and admitting that I was fed–up and sorry for myself. Gradually I fell into silence, and then into something deeper – and suddenly I became aware of something happening to me. I didn't 'hear a voice', but the thought flashed into my mind 'I am love – and you are loved'. It was what later I saw described as a 'peak experience', and it affected me profoundly. I still doubted the worth of what I was engaged upon, still wondered what if anything was to be done about it – but I no longer felt alone, helpless and depressed.

Shortly afterwards there was a welcome change in the administration of IGCR in Italy. The director returned to Britain, and was replaced by his recently–arrived deputy, a Colonel Tomlin who had been Postmaster–General of what used to be known as the Anglo–Egyptian Sudan. We found him business–like and experienced, ready to listen and always constructive. On one occasion, when I had been deploring the negative attitudes of certain officials in the newly–formed UN Relief and Refugee Agency [UNRRA}, he noted in the margin of my report;'Idiot boy!'. I was furious, but when I had cooled off somewhat I went into see him and said 'If you thought I was an idiot boy, sir, I would have appreciated your telling me so face–to–face'. He leaned back in his chair, thought for a few moments, and then smiled broadly. 'My dear Heron, I am terribly sorry: are you not familiar with the expression "idiot boy"?'. Mystified, I said that I was not. He then explained that it was a colloquial term for a negotiating tactic: one pretended ignorance in order to 'draw out' the person from whom one was seeking some appropriate action. Of course I thanked him, and apologised for having misunderstood – and we got on famously thereafter!

Locating and counting

It was agreed that I should make a tour of all camps north of Rome which were reported as holding non–Italian refugees. So off I went again, this time accompanied by a young German refugee. The family of Gerard (26) [and his brother Hans (22)] left Germany before the war, because they realised that their attitude to the Nazi authorities would probably bring trouble upon them. In 1939 the two young men volunteered for the French Foreign Legion, and went to North Africa. At the fall of France in 1940 the Vichy regime deported their parents and transferred the two brothers to forced labour camps near Casablanca. In 1942 Gerard and Hans were employed by a team of the American Friends Service Committee (AFSC), which in 1944 succeeded in arranging for them to be recruited into the British army's Pioneer Corps, from which they were 'detached' for service with IGCR.

Although Gerard was assigned to me as my driver, I preferred to do most of the driving myself, finding him an interesting and loyal comrade on these journeys. He had trained as a teacher, specialising in languages. On this trip, we made a sweep to include Assisi, Perugia, Siena and Florence. As we approached Assisi one morning, after torrential rain the previous days, the truck's windscreen was obliterated by mud, we lurched down and levelled off as I 'hit the brakes'. On getting out from our respective sides we found that we had gone into a shallow shell–crater that I had not noticed! We had a good laugh and went on slowly into the town.

Retreat buildings around the cell (Carcero eremi) of Francos of Assisi

While there we took the opportunity to visit the tomb of Francis, in the crypt beneath the ornate Basilica (to be severely damaged by two earthquake shocks in 1997), and also – much more interesting and moving – the hermitage in the hills known as 'Carcero eremi'. Here I should note how privileged we felt to be able to make such a visit entirely on our own, not as part of a tourist trip.

One day we had stopped to make enquiries at a refugee camp near a town high up in the Appenines, with our next stop Florence. Soon after, we drew up on a flat area where there were hundreds of civilians milling about or sitting in groups. After checking our proposed route, I let in the clutch – and the truck stalled. When this happened a second time, I pulled on the hand brake, and we got out. To our amazement, without either of us noticing, about twenty people had climbed over the tailboard into the empty rear of the truck, complete with their scanty baggage. We had no alternative but to order them out, which they did slowly and with many pleas (in various languages) to be allowed to travel on with us. Once again, I was reminded of our lack of resources or authority, with which to provide at least minimal practical help.

The situation was summarised in a report sent in July 1945 to Bertha Bracey at FRS Refugee Section in London:

*"Avoidance of re–patriation" is on the increase. 'de facto' statelessness **can be** ignored by London and Washington, or at least regarded as a 'problem awaiting clarification' of the political situations in the countries of which such people are nationals; but the consequences here are – as rightly you see them – demoralising. I am far from defeatist, but it is my duty to make it plain that field representatives in Italy are helpless – and know it. It is my serious conviction that the **will** to take a supra–national position, evident to you as existing in IGCR London, is comforting without being adequate to meet a situation which probably can only be solved at UN General Assembly level. Meanwhile, we have **no** positive answer when Military Government and UNRRA Italy ask 'what can IGCR do about such groups?'. What is more, they have no reason to expect that we **shall** have an answer, for a considerable time to come.'*

It was against this background that I began to seek 'a right way forward' for myself as an FRS field worker, bearing in mind earlier agreement that I would return to England at the end of September 1946, to rejoin my wife and children, and take up the university place that I had obtained in Manchester. In the same report as that from which I have just quoted, I wrote:

'The problem as I see it is two–fold. On the one hand, FRS has a limited number of workers, most of whom like myself have a fairly short period free for service abroad. It seems desirable that that these workers should be so disposed by FRS as to render the greatest possible contribution, in face of the overwhelming needs. On the other hand, it can be argued that one year's work gathering information of as yet unassessable value may prove in ten years' time to have been 'equal' to anything more immediate, done in France, Holland or Germany. The danger is, that lacking visible results, and oppressed by the continuous and unrelenting necessity – because of high–level political factors – to say "No: I cannot help you in any way", when

that is the last thing one came overseas to do, one may fail to realise the ultimate value of impersonal work carried out in the midst of unmet need. .... My concern is with the straightforward problem, of achieving maximum usefulness in relation to three factors: alleviable need, FRS resources to meet a very small portion of that need, and the purely personal one of the best use of my family's "widow's mite".'

Vienna – with difficulty

Meanwhile, I suddenly found myself the driver/escort to a senior member of the American organisation pre–eminent in the field of work for Jewish refugees and displaced persons, Morris Beckelman by name, just appointed Assistant–Director of the IGCR. He wanted to consult with active Jewish community workers in Milan, and then go on to Vienna to assess the situation there. Along with the (British) secretary from the Rome office, we arranged to fly to Milan and there pick up my truck which I had left for repairs at the army workshops. We did not know it, but the seeds of trouble had been sown there!

During the journey we stopped for a brew–up at the foot of Lake Garda, and there decided to by–pass Verona by using a secondary road. The usual suspicions attached to such roads were allayed by encouraging evidence of regular use, until a blocked road indicated that the bridge over the Adige River was down. Three (separate) locals assured us that there was a pontoon bridge a few miles ahead, so we pressed on although the road became progressively narrower. Just short of the pontoon bridge, and within sight of the main road on the other side of the river, the engine started to 'pink', and then to knock, so I had to stop. Soon the awful truth was revealed: a careless mechanic had not properly tightened a water seal, and the contents of the radiator were sloshing around inside the cylinder block. We were stuck.

A brief conference had reached the decision that Morris Beckelman would stay with the truck, while the secretary and I tried to get a lift to Bolzano, our destination that evening, and a place where I could arrange for army workshop help. Just then, a small Italian gas–powered truck came along the lane, preparing to cross over the pontoon bridge, The two men with it said they were going to Verona, and offered us a lift in the back. This we accepted, because it was much closer than Bolzano, and there would be a workshop which could send out a recovery vehicle. Thus began the kind of journey one sees in films, as I half sat, half lay amongst the boxes of just–picked grapes in the back. Soon it was twilight, and the little truck chugged along slowly, helped up steep hills by oxen. I ate some grapes, and dozed fitfully, noting in between the dark mountains, the panoply of stars. My other senses were alerted: by the smell of the exhaust, the feel of the sharp edges of the boxes – and the taste of those grapes. We reached Verona at 2330, failed to persuade our hosts to accept payment – just some cigarettes. I shall always think of them as the 'Two gentlemen of Verona'.

Having left the secretary in Milan (on leave), Morris Beckelman and I reached Vienna in due course, having driven 500 miles at 30 mph to run–in the new engine that I had helped to instal at Verona. The city was depressing; severely damaged, the people pale and drawn; no street lighting; most of the remaining shops still shut – and an awareness of much worse to come with winter. Most of the men were not yet back – that is, of those who were still alive to come. Fresh vegetables were not in evidence, and health reports were already pessimistic, despite the efforts of British and American aid agencies. We did not visit the French sector, and would not have been admitted to the Soviet sector had we tried.

I sent a full report to London, raising the question as to whether FRS might decide to become involved in Vienna (or indeed Austria), and indicating my interest and readiness to serve there. Morris Beckelman thought his agency might send him there, and he raised with both IGCR and FRS his wish to have me with him. But they decided that they needed him more somewhere else, so nothing came of this. FRS found itself with more demands upon it than it was able to meet, but decided to send a representative (Richard Rowntree) to Vienna to work with an FAU team.

Return to Britain

My doubts about the rightness of staying with IGCR were not well received in London, but I was in fact rescued through the perceptive understanding of Roger Wilson, who spent a couple of hours with me as he passed through Italy on his way back from a visit to the FRS team in Greece. Having been General Secretary of Friends Relief Service since late 1941, he had moved into the role of Travelling Commissioner. This was a sound decision, for it meant that the realities of the situation for FRS teams and individual workers on the Continent could be conveyed to the committees in London by a responsible and respected eye–witness.

So I arrived back in England in early December 1945, courtesy of RAF Transport Command, and after a short leave with Margaret, was accommodated in one of the London FRS hostels. Somewhat unimaginatively, I was assigned by the small Personnel section to solitary work – all day – in the confined space of a small blanket storeroom, reeking of the anti–moth chemical para–dichlor–benzine. After a fortnight of this, I 'blew my top' and asked to be found some more active occupation. This resulted in a variety of fill–in tasks, including for example scrubbing (on hands and knees) the cockroach–infested floor of the kitchen in the London Hospital medical students hostel, currently occupied by a Friends Ambulance Unit team, This I cheerfully took in my stride, as a positive change from folding blankets !

In January 1946 FRS started assembling a new team for service in northwest Germany. As we reached nearly full strength, getting to know one another as we went along, the others had a meeting at which they decided to put me forward as Team Leader. But they didn't bargain with the power of the two personnel officers at Friends House! Shortly before we were due to leave for the Continent, the last team member arrived and was simultaneously designated as the Team Leader: no arguments. Although in retrospect I could sympathise with head office, where no doubt I had acquired a reputation as an 'awkward customer', later events combined to indicate that an error of judgment had taken place. I remember being rather disappointed (as were several others), but we determined to make the best of it, and give the appointed leader our full backing.

Into Germany

About the end of January we collected our vehicles from an Army base, loaded them up, and in due course landed in the Netherlands. Then we went off in convoy to our destination – in the extreme northwest of Germany, only about 30 miles from the Dutch border to the west, and about 100 miles east of Bremen. We were assigned a fairly large house in a small village called Westerstede, near the city of Oldenburg. Our task was to facilitate the resettlement of German refugees from Silesia, displaced by the advancing Soviet forces. They came in trainloads, with what they could carry. It quickly became very obvious that they were not at all welcome. The northern part of Land Oldenburg was a rich farming area, and it had experienced little hardship, no bombing. Many of the people spoke a dialect called 'Platt Deutsch'. closely related to Dutch.

We decided to set up simple workshops (clothing, footwear, artrificial limbs, furniture) to give the refugees meaningful occupation. As we had no supplies at our disposal, I presented myself to the officer in charge of a Canadian Army surplus stores depot,

'All their worldly goods', with which to start 'a new life'

and agreed with him what we could have for the taking. One of the best hauls was a truckload of army boots – but I was glad to take a wide variety of less–obviously useable stuff. such as the useful wood from packing cases. The team

was able to step up the production of artificial limbs to eight per week. Winter driving conditions were hard and potentially dangerous, mainly because of the dome–topped cobbled roads, most with ditches at each side, backed by rows of poplars.

FRS team members in workshop, started to enable salvaged wood and leather to be made into serviceable articles for 'expellees'

It was good to be at last engaged in work for which I had originally volunteered, and to be a member of a team with a specific job to do. Looking back, I have to recognise that I was lacking in tolerance for the divergent views of two or three members of the team. They had little or no previous experience with Quakers, and had been accepted for service mainly on the basis of relevant skills. Understandably, they tended to be impatient with the short daily Quaker 'meeting for worship', based on silence – and even more with our practice of reaching decisions without the use of votes. But most of the time we managed, and the work got done. Happily, there were occasions for humour.

One of the team, fully committed to increasing his ability to discuss things in German with the locals, tended to fall into the well–known trap of saying 'Ja, ja' ('Yes, yes') when in fact he had not fully understood what had been said to him. The result was that the team had a wholly unexpected 'state visit' from the mayor and council of a village in our area – and some very hasty improvisations were needed to provide appropriate hospitality! One story against myself involved the Canadian major from the surplus stores depot. I had arranged with the team to fetch him to our house for a meal and some exchange of ideas. For some reason or other, the subject of my 'fast driving' came up, at which I protested 'But I never drive faster than fifty!'; in a flash he quipped ' And seldom less!'

A Brigadier from British Military Government had his office and residence in our small town, so we of course invited him over along with his local staff, on more than one occasion. Through this I got to know the two young German women secretaries, and was invited by them to join them for an evening, partly to listen to records of classical music. One outcome was their wish to hear readings from Shakespeare, so in due course I acceded to this request – apparently quite acceptably! They particularly enjoyed the Sonnets,

Delivering a bath, to help 175 'expellees' fight scabies (though without real soap or a change of clothing)

I remember. One of them later came to Manchester to stay with the family while Margaret and I went on the 'Grand Tour' [see later], and then to type my MSc thesis; we have kept in touch ever since, visiting her twice in Germany.

I also came to know well one of the refugees from Silesia, who had arrived on one of the trains from the East. He had lost a leg on the German army's Russian campaign, but was otherwise fairly well, and eventually we were able to set him up in a small house as a sort of jobbing tailor. But the great day was when his wife, from whom he had been separated back east in the camps, where men and women were held in different places, suddenly turned up on one of the trains. Joy was indeed unconfined!

In addition to our Army 3–ton truck and a pair of 15–hundredweights, we had two large 'box–on–wheels' ambulances with the Quaker Star painted on the sides, instead of the usual red cross, one of which was assigned to me. It was only rarely used for its original purpose, but on one occasion I made a long journey down to

An FRS 'box–on–wheels' ambulance with the Quaker Star painted on the side in Germany (1946)

Gottingen, accompanied by my usual team–mate Enid Barkas. This was to take a very sick man to the University Polyclinic there, in the rather forlorn hope that they could do something for him. When we arrived at the hospital, Enid and I presented ourselves to the reception office, to which a doctor was soon called. In fluent German, Enid explained that we had been asked by the medical authorities in Oldenburg to bring this patient to Gottingen. I noticed the doctor eyeing our grey uniforms, and the Quaker Star badge on our berets, but the *pièce de resistance* came at the end of Enid's explanations. 'What part of Germany do you come from?', he asked her: 'Here', she replied, 'I'm British, but I grew up here in Gottingen'. You could have knocked him down with the proverbial feather! (Enid's father had been the English 'dozent' at the University of Gottingen, until it was no longer safe for him and his family to remain in Germany).

On another trip, not so long, to the Hamburg area, I was able to locate the farm where lived the parents of our refugee office secretary in Bari, and give them her address. It was the first time that they knew her to be still alive.

I was only eight months with the team (which shortly afterwards moved into Oldenburg, and was joined by two new members from the American Friends Service Committee (AFSC), but I found the experience fulfilling. Despite the team's internal difficulties, largely surmounted, it was a happy time in which much was shared. On reflection, I doubt whether we made much of a specifically Quaker impact, but I think the team did a useful piece of work, unglamorous as it was. Approaching my thirty–first birthday, I had gained in breadth through an unusual variety of experiences, but less in spiritual depth despite some 'openings'. But I was aware of foundations, upon which I would be called to build; and I had just enough humility to recognise that I must always be ready to be changed – not just through further experience of life, but inwardly through the leadings of the Spirit.

4 A fresh start

The Manchester years

Before leaving in February 1945 for Italy, I had obtained the firm offer of a place in the University of Manchester, to study psychology. On that basis, we bought a Victorian house (cellars, ground floor, second floor, and attic rooms) near Alexandra Park (Whalley Range) in Manchester. In December 1944 I had fetched Marg and the children from the Gaudies, and established them in our new home. I also arranged for them to be joined by a resident helper, a young woman aged about 16 whom I had met when working briefly for FRS at Chaigeley School, in north Lancashire. She was a refugee from Liverpool, and the school was concerned that she go to a suitable residential job on leaving. She stayed with us until her marriage in (I think) 1952. We have remained in touch ever since, and Mary became a Quaker after her family grew up. We had or obtained just about enough basic furniture to enable Margaret to take a lodger (a woman medical student), so I was able to feel that she and the children were not being left to fend for themselves (with the war still in progress).

When I arrived in Manchester to start at the University, at the beginning of October 1946, and the household was further increased by the arrival of Vic Chase (a fellow–student from Birkbeck, starting a medical course), the 'group dynamics' of the domestic situation became somewhat tense. It was far from easy for three women, plus two children aged 4 and 3, to adapt their established pattern of life to accommodate two strange men! I recall my own readiness to adapt as very much less than satisfactory, but Marg coped extremely well with us all and we managed. We were very fortunate in finding nursery class places for both the children, and then later places at Wythenshawe Primary School – where our friend Kath Gamble welcomed Keith and Joy in successive years into her 'admissions class'. Later we took more lodgers, including Joan (later Heald), Sue (later Scrivener), and Muriel (to whom Vic was later married).

My university course was for an MSc degree, even though I did not have a BSc, only my Diploma from Birkbeck, where work for my degree was interrupted by my departure to FRS and then overseas. This very favourable arrangement – to proceed straight to a Master's degree by course work and research – was made possible by the fact that the University of Manchester had made provision before and during the war for Jewish and other refugees from Nazi oppression, by adding a clause to the MSc regulations. If one proceeded to a master's degree by research in the **same** subject as one's (British) honours degree, it took only one year; if in a **different** subject, two years; and (the extra clause) in three years (with a programme of approved course work) if one did not hold a British honours degree at all.

So I enrolled for courses in philosophy (modern, with ethics), and (in the Medical School) in the anatomy and physiology of the central nervous system. These were additional to my full programme of courses in the Dept of Psychology. Life in the university immediately after the war was of course very different from that experienced by students coming straight from school – of whom in 1946 there were relatively few. Our ages ranged from the early 20s to the middle 30s, and our wartime experiences were still fresh in our minds. There was a strong sense among the older ones of 'trying to make up for lost time', so people worked hard and made very 'adult ' demands upon the teaching staff. Sometimes the lecturer was thrown on the defensive, as questioning minds refused to simply take what said as 'gospel'.

This could be funny or serious, as two examples may show. I was one of a small group taking statistics, which involved the teacher in quite a lot of writing formulas on the blackboard. One afternoon, while he was doing this, a voice from the back row said, quietly but distinctly, 'I'm sorry, sir, but what you just wrote is incorrect'. The lecturer swivelled round, and asked who had spoken; our fellow–student lifted his hand. 'What is incorrect?' came the question; the student courteously explained. As I was sitting in the front row, I was just able to hear the lecturer murmur *sotto voce* 'My God! and I've been writing that for 18 years'.

In a different group taking ethics, we faced every week a tutor who used the draft of his projected textbook as his teaching medium, seldom raising his head from reading sections of it to us. After some weeks of this, I must have run out of patience, and suddenly exclaimed 'But sir, that didn't follow from what you said just before!'. Unfortunately, he couldn't field this one, and had to ask 'What went before?' and look at his draft text. Other students joined in, and we had a short discussion. The next week we were all waiting as usual for him to appear – he was usually very punctual – but he came in late, wearing his black gown, sat down and, without raising his head, announced 'There is to be no further discussion during these lectures'. Of course, we were convulsed, but managed to stifle our reactions.

But there was a surprising sequel. When he returned the essays that we had written during the mid–term break, he said 'These are better than I had expected: but I think we could benefit from some discussion'. All credit to him!

In due course, I decided to carry out a research project in 'education for parenthood': this needs an explanation! For my own part, I had already come to realise how ill–equipped I was to be a parent myself, and to wonder whether it might be possible to introduce some basic 'preparation' in secondary schools. I did not have mainly in mind the practical aspects of parenthood – though these would not be neglected – but more the whole question of attitude to the role, and to equal sharing between the two parents.

I soon found that there was effectively no previous work in this area in Britain, and only very little in the USA. When I came to seek facilities in schools, I was met by open amazement that 'a **man** was doing it'! However, I did succeed in carrying out two substantial school surveys, the first in Devon, the second in Oldham, Lancashire. My published results showed that boys as well as girls were prepared to be interested around the age of 15 years: this received no attention until well into the 1980s, when a Birmingham research group borrowed a copy of my MSc thesis, had me to meet them, and made use of the findings in planning their own studies. The topic had to wait until the middle 1990s before being taken seriously, so I was almost fifty years too soon.

In the course of analysing the results, some of the material serendipitously threw fresh light on personality in adolescence, and I published a separate paper on that. This side of the work – and my analysis and conclusions – aroused the interest of my external examiner for the thesis: Hans Eysenck, at the Maudsley Hospital in London. This led him to suggest my name to Professor (later Sir) Aubrey Lewis, who needed a psychologist for an off–shoot to the Medical Research Council unit of which he was the Honorary Director. I should have mentioned earlier that my three–years course at the university was covered by a government Postwar Grant, for which my time in the London Rescue Service had made me eligible. For a married man with two children, this was £337 a year, so we had to make do with that and the small income from our student lodgers. We kept very detailed accounts (my previous experience ensured that), and found that we had ended the three years in Dickensian style, about £10 in the black. So when I was offered an interview with Aubrey Lewis in London, I hitch–hiked there from Manchester. On getting my first appointment – for one year – with the Medical Research Council, at £600, I came back by coach!

Hans Eysenck, six months younger than myself, was a pre-war refugee from Germany. He obtained his doctorate in psychology at University College London under Sir Cyril Burt, and then joined the staff of the Institute of Psychiatry at the Maudsley Hospital, where he spent the whole of his working life. The author of about sixty books and hundreds of scientific papers, he was probably the psychologist best known to the British public. Although he was twice honoured by the American Psychological Association, the Council of the British Psychological Society failed to do the same. He was a controversial figure, perhaps mostly because of his penetrating attacks on the theoretical basis of Freudian psycho–analysis. During my fourteen years with the Medical Research Council we saw each other fairly often, and I enjoyed my friendship with him and his second wife Dr Sybil Eysenck. Although we lost touch while I was abroad, and met only occasionally after my return to Britain, I was able to take part in a commemorative evening after his death in the latter part of 1997, when several speakers – in my view rightly – described him as 'a giant in psychological science'.

If I had not gone to the MRC, almost certainly I would have become a tutor in the Extra–Mural Department of the University of Leeds. During the three years of my Manchester course, I had been caught up in the post–war boom in demand for informal adult education. This was met with difficulty by the Workers Educational Association, and the extra–mural departments of universities. Among the most popular subjects psychology was prominent, so I found myself as a graduate student facing large classes of enthusiastic adults, from a great variety of educational and social backgrounds. It turned out that

I had some aptitude for this kind of informal teaching, so I had become known to some of those experienced in this field. I also served as the chairman of the Manchester area Tutors Association.

A full-time job

Although the MRC unit directed by Aubrey Lewis was based at the Maudsley Hospital in London, my appointment was as the psychologist in a three–man team to work in Manchester. The two others were a psychiatrist and an economist, so I was pitched straight into the sometimes murky waters of multi–disciplinary cooperation. Our task was to gain entry into factories and other situations where it would be possible to study systematically the extent to which people of below–average intelligence, or suffering from psychotic or neurotic illness, were occupationally disadvantaged. Our first working base was in the factory producing Exide batteries. This had been made possible through the pioneering work there, over many years, on the prevention of lead poisoning, carried out by the company's Medical Officer, Ronald Lane, who had just been appointed Professor and the Director of the new Nuffield Department of Occupational Health in the University. Subsequently we also carried out research in one of the Ferranti plants, and later I did a one–man project within Manchester Corporation Transport (which I was able to replicate in London Transport).

The early 1950s became known as 'the era of full employment', in which unemployment reached a peace–time low point. While that meant that we were likely to find appropriate 'subjects' for our enquiries, their potential 'occupational disadvantage' was likely to be reduced. So while we could show that many of them were capable of carrying out unskilled and semi–skilled jobs successfully, we could not determine what might be the negative effects of a less favourable 'employment market'. We were in fact studying a 'marginal population'.

Our team was an odd assortment, to put it mildly. Neither of my colleagues had research experience; the psychiatrist quite naturally tended to assume medical superiority while the economist, with a background of work for the Milk Marketing Board, perceived his role as one of 'keeping our feet on the ground'. But fortunately they were both very nice men, in their very different ways, and we managed fairly well. I was very fortunate in being able, as a part–time graduate student of Birkbeck College, to use my fieldwork material in my thesis for the PhD degree. Subsequently I published three scientific papers based upon this work, followed by others arising from some of the workplace projects.

The other member of the team was our secretary Hilda Jackson, a true 'Lancashire lass'. Our family established an enduring friendship with her, and during the late 1980s and through the 1990s Margaret and I have joined her family and close friends in annual New Year's Day festivities, in her home in the Pennines above Hebden Bridge – a converted late Tudor stone–built hall.

While still at the University in Manchester I had become involved in many and varied activities, and some of these continued to make calls upon my time and energies. Among them was the local branch of the then very young and small trades union the Association of Scientific Workers. Most of my fellow–members were technicians in university or industrial laboratories, and several of the most active were members of the Communist Party. I had no leanings in that direction, but somewhat to my surprise found myself elected as Chairman of the branch committee. It gradually dawned on me that I was perceived by many of the members as the obvious person to 'keep the Communists in check', while still actively pursuing agreed objectives in such familiar matters as pay and working conditions. I worked quite hard as chairman, and in fact only stood down when the leading Communist activists decided that their aims could be served more effectively somewhere else.

During the winter months I served as the tutor of two 'tutorial classes' organised by the Workers Educational Association, both designed to last three winter sessions. Of these, one was located in Burnley, then a thriving city in the cotton spinning and weaving industry. So I had cotton workers in my class – and they taught me how to teach adults. One of them, who always sat in the front row, rarely took part in the discussion that occupied the second of our two hours weekly. But on one occasion, when I had been trying to explain some basic point in elementary statistics, she suddenly said in broad Lancashire 'I don't know what you mean!'. The ball was clearly in my court, so I paused for a few moments, and then approached the point in a different way. At the end of my fresh attempt, she nodded, so I then brought the rest of the class into discussion of the matter. Her intervention encouraged others, and more people gained the confidence to 'stop me in mid–flight' in subsequent sessions of the class.

During the winter of 1950–51 I began to suffer from migraine attacks, severe though without the nausea and sickness that is often a feature of the condition. Frequently, I would come home from work, miss my evening meal and go off to the bedroom to rest in darkness. On my WEA nights it became a matter of hoping to recover in time to drive twenty miles each way, with the 2–hours class in between. Naturally, I consulted my medical colleague, who arranged for me to have some tests. These only served to confirm that it was indeed migraine. One afternoon we were alone in our small shared office, working back–to–back at our respective desks. I took the opportunity to ask him how long I could expect to remain subject to migraine attacks: we swung round to face each other, and then he said 'They tend to ease off around fifty'. Startled, I exclaimed 'Do you really mean that I must face nearly twenty years of this?' – to which he replied simply 'Yes'. We turned back to our work.

Some minutes later, I said 'I'm sorry to interrupt you again – but what if anything can I do about this?'. He took his time before responding, then said 'As far as I am aware, there are only two possibilities, and they are of course related'. I waited, and he went on 'You might go through an especially successful psycho–analysis, but that's a course I wouldn't recommend. The alternative would be to experience what is usually described as a religious conversion'. We sat silent for some minutes before I managed to say 'You mean that my personality would need to change, don't you?', to which he nodded assent. We again returned to our work, after I had thanked him for his directness. I was genuinely humbled, made conscious of what a short distance I had travelled on my spiritual journey in fifteen years. But I also felt grateful that my Jewish colleague had been so faithful a transmitter of that message.

Naturally I told Margaret about this, and enlisted her ready support in my search for insight and change. I also mentioned it to some members of the Quaker meeting in which we were active, not least because I perceived the problem as basically spiritual. Gradually I came to recognise that I was engaged on a fruitless attempt to 'make up', academically and professionally, for the late start at the age of 34. Not only was I working 'flat out' at my MRC job, but I was almost feverishly active in other directions, including serving as chairman or secretary of various bodies or committees. Most significantly, I was almost incapable of saying 'No' when asked to take on something that I thought I could do well. It was borne in upon me that my first step was to accept that I was, quite bluntly, *not indispensable.* More positively, I was challenged to recover the practice of daily seeking the guidance of the Holy Spirit in every aspect of my life. It would be a slow business, but I had enough faith in the love of God to believe that change was possible.

About two years later I found myself strolling after lunch with my psychiatrist colleague, who had been transferred to our main unit in London some months previously. Eventually, he asked me quietly 'And how are the migraines these days?'. I replied 'Thanks to your good honest advice, I am free of them'. A usually undemonstrative man, he stopped abruptly in his tracks and exclaimed 'But how?' – to which I could only reply 'Through the change in my personality that was necessary'. And I told him the story.

Back to the job – and on a lighter note. Having obtained the agreement of both management and the trades union for a study of new recruits as bus conductors, I asked for cooperation in preparing myself to carry out the work. It seemed to me essential that I have at least some brief experience of the job itself, so I arranged to be included in the initial training of a batch of recruits. In those days, the conductor collected the fares by moving through the bus (on both lower and upper decks), as well as being responsible for signalling the driver to move away from the bus–stops. It was a disadvantage to be tall, especially as the uniform included a flat–topped peaked cap. I spent most of my time in a half–crouched position! I managed to put in a fortnight on the job without my 'cover being blown' – and without being spotted by a passenger who recognised me. Our children (then aged 8 and 9) thought it was a great lark!

That reminds me of the earlier occasion when our daughter Joy was in a bus on her way to school, unaware that her teacher was on the same bus. In one of those unexpected lulls in the general buzz of noise, Joy was asked by her little classmate 'What does your Daddy do?' – so everybody waited for the answer. After a pause, Joy replied 'He works in a factory', but immediately added 'No – he watches other people work'. Hilarity in the bus.

Working (incognito) as a bus conductor in Manchester (1952)

Keith and Joy above Wastwater during a family holiday in 1949

During the summers of 1947 and 1948, I took part in two of the first post–war summer schools, held in the German universities of Bonn and Gottingen. The German students were, like ourselves, mostly war veterans. At Gottingen, I was told that a psychology student very much wanted to meet me, but it would have to be in his lodgings, as he had lost both legs during the siege of Stalingrad. So I went along – and spent most of the night talking with him. The long–term outcome was his later arrival in London, as a postgraduate student under Hans Eysenck at the Institute of Psychiatry, where we met again and then kept in touch. He eventually became a distinguished member of the scientific staff of the Max Planck Institute in Munich.

The 'Grand Tour'

Early in our Manchester days, I had promised Margaret that I would, before her fortieth birthday, take her to every place where I had served with FRS in 1945–46. So in the summer of 1952, when there were severe restrictions on the amount of money that could be taken out of Britain, we spent six weeks fulfilling my promise – of which only twelve nights were **not** spent under canvas. Starting in the northern Netherlands, we travelled south through Germany, through Austria and the Brenner Pass into Italy. From Venice we followed the Adriatic coast right down to the tip of the 'heel' of Italy, at Santa Maria de Leuca. There it turned out that we were the first Britishers they had seen since the troops left seven years previously.

The way back was through the mountains of Calabria (including the village where I had learned that the war in Europe was over), to Salerno, Positano and Naples, thence north to Rome. We did a loop to visit Assisi and Perugia ('the jewel of Umbria') before going up the Italian and French Rivieras, then north–west through France into Belgium. Our last night was of necessity spent in the dunes outside the Channel resort of Le Zoute. There we were asked during the night by the police to 'remove ourselves from the garden of M. le Maire'. Remaining firmly in my sleeping bag, I explained in French the nature of our predicament, and undertook to be away soon after dawn. Eventually they agreed, and we went back to sleep. (It wasn't 'his garden' by the way – though no doubt the sand dune formed part of his property!).

Those were good years in Manchester, and our children enjoyed and benefitted from the 'extended' family of our student lodgers, who all became close friends, with whom we have kept in touch through the years. For a time this family provided a home for a Polish refugee, who for security reasons had to take on (officially) a new identity. This worked out very happily, and 'Bill' went on to a successful life, in both family and occupational terms – and we are still in touch. We also greatly valued our participation in the life of our Quaker meeting at Wythenshawe. During the winter months we had a fortnightly Sunday evening gathering at our house for 'younger Friends' and some interested students. We discussed a wide range of topics – Quaker, religious, philosophical, topical – and formed a fellowship that was recalled many years later when we met afresh some of those who had taken part.

Back south – and a trip to North America

I had been joined in Manchester by a psychology graduate from University College London, who previously had been in the Royal Navy. This was Peter Venables, who like me acquired a Birkbeck PhD through our Manchester work. He went on later to a distinguished career, first at Birkbeck where he became a professor, and then as the foundation professor of psychology at the new University of York. By the end of 1952 I was the only member of the research staff remaining in Manchester, and in 1953 was transferred to London, to join the main unit at the Maudsley Hospital. We found a bungalow on the road to Westerham in Kent, near Biggin Hill where the RAF still had a fighter station. Yes: it was very noisy at times. In the summer of 1954 the Medical Research Council sent me to the USA and eastern Canada, to visit many research departments and institutes. I went out on the liner Queen Elizabeth, and returned by air – at that time a novel experience, I was also able to attend two international conferences, to which I presented papers based on my MRC work, These were held in Montreal and in Toronto.

As soon as I had shed my luggage on arrival in Montreal, I set off to visit my old school. As it was during the summer vacation, I did not expect to find many people about, but I went in the front door and started to look around,

Then a door opened and a lady came out, who asked me if she could be of any assistance. I replied that I doubted it, since I was a former pupil from 23 years previously! She asked my name, then said 'Just wait a minute, please', and went back to her office. Then another door flew open – and out came the current Rector, the same man who had been in charge of the Cadet Corps in my day. Hand outstretched, he greeted me 'Heron – how good to see you again!'. He whisked me up to the nearly empty cafeteria, where we found two masters who had taught me: it was quite a re–union.

During the Toronto conference I was offered a senior appointment in South Africa, with its well–known institute devoted to occupational psychology. I was pleased at the offer, but quite clear in my mind that it could not be accepted. I doubted whether I would last more than a few months in the country, before being encouraged to leave, or actually deported – and said so frankly. The regime of 'apartheid' was not one in which Margaret and I could have lived without 'getting into trouble'.

I was amazed to find at the conference my chief, Aubrey Lewis, since he was well–known for his view that they were usually a waste of time! But it turned out that he had suffered some heart trouble, and was told firmly by his physicians to 'take a holiday out of Britain somewhere' – so he compromised by a sea–voyage and an international conference. We were in the same hall of residence, and one evening I found myself standing side–by–side with him at the basins, washing our nylon shirts: this was certainly a new relationship! Knowing by reliable hearsay of his addiction to good films, I ventured to ask if he might like to go with me to a film in which a real actress (from the theatre) was the star (Anna Magnani). He agreed, and off we went the next evening, after an appropriate Italian meal. When we were walking back afterwards, I asked him what he thought of the film, and found that he had enjoyed it very much – greatly to my relief! I had noticed a rustling noise, and shortly afterwards he pulled a paper bag out of his pocket, and said 'Have a cherry'.

He had a fearsome reputation for demolishing 'medics who hadn't done their homework', and was certainly a tough opponent in our unit discussions about the research we were doing, or proposed doing. But even without the Toronto experience, I always respected and got along well with him. Years later, when

82

he heard that I had gone out to Zambia, he was reported as commenting 'Heron always was an idealist'.

In between the conferences, I was able to participate in an historic Quaker event. Despite their relatively small numbers, Quakers in Canada for historical reasons had remained in three separate Yearly Meetings. Following much patient preliminary work, agreement had been reached that in the summer of 1954 there would be a joint gathering, at which the possibility of uniting in a single yearly meeting could be considered. I was made very welcome, especially by the group of Young Friends (in spite of my age!), and en-couraged to attend all the meetings. Several of these were understandably difficult, and feelings ran deep among the older members. But by the end of the week, agreement was reached between the two larger groups that a new 'Canadian Yearly Meeting' should come into being the following year. The few isolated local meetings that belonged to the third grouping decided to go their own ways. It was not until seeking the names of those in the accompanying photograph, 44 years later, that I was given a copy of a minute from that occasion:

'Friends expressed their sense of indebtedness to Alastair Heron, for his invaluable contribution by way of counsel and inspiration, in the sessions of our Yearly Meetings.'

In early 1954 Joy was offered a place in the then Sadlers Wells ballet school; this led to my meeting one afternoon (in a very small room) with three ladies, to seek their advice. One was the ballet mistress, another the person responsible for general education – and the third was Ninette de Valois. They said frankly that though people in ballet traditionally referred to 'ballet mothers', it was a novelty to meet a 'ballet father'! They were forthcoming and very helpful, and I was able to feed in what I had learned to the discussions at home. Two things were clear, both of which related to physical development.

Yonge Street Quaker Meeting House, Ontario, Canada

First, exercise in the school programme was of necessity planned to be consistent with the needs of dancing: for example, bicycle–riding was unsuitable. Second, it had to be understood that in spite of all precautions, physical development would vary from one girl to another, and sometimes by the age of 16 or 17 it became obvious that ballet was not the right career.

Family life

We were by then just becoming used to our monthly 'family council', where matters put on the agenda by any of us would be considered, On the day that Joy had to decide about the ballet school offer, we sat quietly as usual. Then her brother Keith asked Joy how she felt about it. After a long pause she replied 'I think I want to be an ordinary girl'. This settled the matter, since the prime requirement was that she wanted above all other considerations to be a ballet dancer. We were agreed as a family that she should turn down the offer – and she has never regretted doing so.

Back at the Maudsley with the unit, increasingly I found it difficult to see my way forward within the research policy that had been adopted. Each of my colleagues had identified a particular line that looked promising, and were actively at work. I was not unduly worried, because I had the feeling that a little patience would not be amiss, and that I would also see a fresh objective. By this time, we had settled down in our new home, and Keith and Joy were happy and doing well at their respective state grammar schools in Beckenham. I was an elder in the Quaker meeting at Bromley, which we all attended on Sunday mornings. It began to look as though life was about to become quieter, as I moved towards my fortieth birthday.

At Pickering College, Ontario: with the Clerks of the separate Yearly Meetings in Canada, and representatives from USA Quaker bodies (1954)
l-r Sylvan Warren, Errol Elliott, Bertha Pollard, Howard Clayton, Mable Willson, Stirling Nelson, Grace Mekeel, Leonard Hall,?, Alastair Heron

5 Ups and downs

Back to the north-west

I could hardly have been more mistaken. Out of the blue came an invitation from the professor of psychology at the University of Liverpool, Leslie Hearnshaw, to discuss a proposal. He had agreed with the Medical Research Council to serve as the honorary director of a new Unit for Research in Occupational Aspects of Ageing, to be based in his department. As he could not take this on full–time, he was seeking a full–time deputy director who would effectively be in charge of the day–to–day work of the unit – and he was offering me this appointment.

Margaret and I asked two of our fellow–members of the Quaker meeting in Bromley to 'sit with us', while together we sought the leading of the Spirit about our immediate future. We also sat quietly with our children, now aged 12 and 11, since a move to the Liverpool area would face them with adjustment to new schools. The outcome was felt to be clear to us all: that it was right for me to accept the invitation.

In due course, we found a suitable house in the village of Heswall, in the Wirral peninsula across the River Mersey from Liverpool, and places for Keith and Joy in the separate single–gender state grammar schools. On 1 October 1955 I started my new job, which would involve decisions on an initial programme of research, the recruitment of staff, and the use of MRC 'start–up' funds for the purchase of basic laboratory equipment. The unit was to be located in the house next door to the department, to which a connecting door would be provided.

We found a small group of Quakers in the Heswall area, without a meeting house. They met on Sunday mornings in a rented tin shack, heated in winter by gas fires. It consisted of a single room about twenty feet long by fifteen feet wide, and a tiny cubby–hole room in which to prepare simple refreshments. The accommodation was not very inviting to newcomers, however warm the personal welcome, and the lack of accommodation for a children's class was a major disadvantage. Heswall Meeting did not acquire a purpose–built meeting house until about mid–1965, two years after our family had left the Wirral.

Margaret and I were two of the handful of Friends that worked its way slowly to a conviction that it was right to commission an architect, and then to go ahead with the building. Although our children took part in events arranged by the group of local meetings to which Heswall belonged (the Monthly Meeting), and went to Summer Schools and (later) work camps, they certainly 'missed–out' on the basic regular experience of the Quaker meeting for worship.

Their two schools could hardly have differed more: Keith gained, and Joy lost by their move from the south. In the boys school, parents were actively encouraged to be involved; music and drama flourished; and overall it was an exciting place with high academic standards and generally good teaching. Joy's school in the south had three choirs and two orchestras, and parents were welcome. Her new school was conventional in the extreme, curriculum–bound and without organised provision for music. As to the parents: when Margaret and I visited the school prior to our move, the interview with the headmistress ended – when we were already on our feet – with my asking 'Do you have a parent–teacher association?'. The headmistress (in Margaret's words later) 'looked straight through Alastair as if he wasn't there', and said to Margaret 'We have a meeting with the **mothers** at the beginning of each term'.

Heron Family 1959

Keith and Joy both did well in the O–level examinations, and went on in their respective Sixth Forms to prepare for the A–level hurdle. In addition to his physics, chemistry and biology. Keith had also taken and passed the new 'General' paper, and in the following year Joy proposed taking it – but her school **refused to enter her!** When Joy pressed her case, and asked why she was not to be entered, the deputy headmistress replied 'The school cannot risk your failing: it would reflect on our reputation'. When Joy reported this at home, she accepted my offer to write a letter in which I would politely but firmly exercise our right to enter her ourselves, paying the examination fee. They caved in and entered her; she passed with a good grade, in addition to her three other subjects.

Research on ageing

From the outset, I had determined to strike a balance between work in the laboratory and work 'in the field'. In our first phase, the latter included a major survey of attitudes to the employment of 'older workers' in manufacturing industry. I sought the cooperation of 24 firms on Merseyside, one from each of the categories listed in the census of occupations – only one refused: Tate and Lyle (the sugar refiners). We were able to establish that while men and women over 50 years of age were generally valued for their good timekeeping, low absenteeism and conscientious work, they tended not to be recruited because of the widespread assumption that 'you cannot teach old dogs new tricks'. Retirement was usually compulsory at the state pensionable ages of 65 for men, 50 for women.

Our laboratory work started mainly with auditory and visual perception, and later concentrated on reasoning and on short–term and immediate memory. Having noticed that almost all systematic research on human ageing had been carried out by comparison of groups of younger and of older subjects, with little or no attempt to equate the age–groups on other relevant criteria, I decided to create a pool of subjects in the Liverpool area. To reduce the self–selective consequences of seeking volunteers, I sought opportunities, in a wide range of settings, to address large groups of employees, members of clubs and societies, etc. Having explained our needs, and that we would not call upon anyone more often than twice in a year, to come to the unit (travelling expenses paid), I sought to obtain the cooperation of the whole group, while recognising the right of any individual present to 'contract out'. While the proportion 'contracting out' varied, overall I obtained a much less self–selected subject population to serve as our subjects for study. Soon after I had met with each group, those agreeing to join our 'research panel' were called in by appointment, to undertake tests of verbal and non–verbal reasoning ability, emotional stability, and temperament. Members of the unit were then able to make up groups for experimental projects according to age, that were matched in terms of one or more of these criteria.

Later on, I made up a 'synthetic population' strictly representative of the Registrar General's five 'socio–economic' groupings, consisting of 50 men and 40 women in each of the six decades of the lifespan, 20s to 70s inclusive. The whole of this population served as the subjects for a detailed investigation of the changes in physical, physiological and psychological functioning in relation to chronological age. The results of this pioneering study were published in 1967, in a book prepared jointly by a member of the unit (Sheila Chown) and myself, under the title *Age and function.* It showed that not only do the various functions vary differently with age from one individual to another, but also that the amount of change of different functions varies from function to function *within* the same individual. So, for example, one person aged sixty may be relatively young in terms of hearing, while at the same time relatively old in terms of non–verbal reasoning ability, while typical for short–term memory recall. Overall, the chronological age of a person is a very unsatisfactory basis upon which to make a match with the demands of a particular occupation or job. Thirty years later this is still ignored, at great cost both to the thousands of men and women made unemployable, and to the economy through wastage of skills and experience.

In those days, there were very few research projects into the processes of normal ageing, even fewer with a main emphasis on the psychological aspects. With the aid of an occasional conference, and some visits, those of us who were involved came to know one another personally, and in some cases (such as Jim and Betty Birren in California) became close friends, remaining in contact over the years and taking opportunities for mutual home visits.

I should note in passing that from 1956 to 1963 I served as Honorary Treasurer of the British Psychological Society. It can fairly be said that it moved from near–insolvency to a modest but sound financial position in that period. Perhaps my training and experience in accountancy had been enabled to find an appropriate application. Much as I enjoyed the challenges of those years, I do have to admit that subsequently I made a point of keeping my accountancy 'under wraps', thus avoiding treasurer roles with great success!

A time for decision

In 1958 I replaced Leslie Hearnshaw as director of the unit, which came to consist of twelve full–time and four part–time staff. At all times I continued as an active research worker, usually in cooperation with another member of the team. By 1962 the unit had published a good number of scientific papers, and we were coming to the end of data–gathering in the 'functional age' project. It was time to look to the future, which would of course be determined by the Medical Research Council. Members of the unit were united in thinking that future work should include the initiation of a longitudinal study, that would make possible the recording of changes in the **same** individuals over time. The weakness of almost all previous work, including our own, lay in the attempt to demonstrate and measure change by comparing groups of **different** individuals at a single point in time. We were also clear that such a study would of necessity involve cooperation with local doctors and with hospitals, within the National Health Service.

The Council did not see its way to support this proposal for the unit, while not having any positive alternative to suggest. Most of us started looking for suitable appointments elsewhere. About that time, the Vice–Chancellor of my old university in Manchester (Professor Mansfield Cooper) asked me to come and see him. It turned out that they were in a position to create a new chair in adult education, and he wanted to know if I might be interested. In the circumstances, I was – so in due course I was invited to meet with the university's search committee: some time later the Vice–Chancellor said that I was the first choice of the committee, and that he would get in touch with me when the matter came before the university Council, probably early in the New Year.

One morning in early December, I was idly casting my eye over the advertisements for academic appointments in *The Guardian*, when my attention was caught by the word 'Africa'. This entry concerned the appointment of a director for the Rhodes–Livingstone Institute, in what was then Northern Rhodesia, which had become part of the Federation of Rhodesia and Nyasaland. Apparently the Institute had been taken over by the new University College, situated in Salisbury, capital of Southern Rhodesia and of the Federation. The advertisement specified that the appointment was intended to be multi–disciplinary in orientation, so applications were invited from persons with qualifications and experience in any of the social sciences.

More than once in the past, Margaret and I had wondered if way would ever open for us to be of some service in an African country (other than South Africa), so she encouraged me to apply for the post. Just before Christmas, I was called to London, to be interviewed by a small panel set up by a body called the Inter–University Council for Universities Overseas. I found myself ushered into a large room in a house in Bloomsbury, that contained a chair for me positioned about fifteen feet from a long table, covered with green baize, behind which sat the panel. There was no other furniture in the room. At the end of a fairly uneventful session, the man in the chair asked me if I had any points that I would like to raise: I had.

Having 'done my homework', I was very aware that the Federation was thought unlikely to survive, and that indigenous movements in both Nyasaland and Northern Rhodesia were actively seeking independence. Having made clear my awareness to the panel, I suggested that – in the event of my being offered the appointment when the report had been considered in Salisbury – there was a strong case for me to go out there 'to see and be seen'. There was a measurable silence, and then the anthropologist member (Schapera, from Oxford) thanked me for making the suggestion, which he proposed the panel should bear in mind. I went off fairly sure that I would **not** be offered the job, to have lunch with Margaret, Keith and Joy, and a close friend from Manchester days – Richard Schilling, professor of occupational medicine in the nearby London School of Hygiene and Tropical Medicine.

Back at work in Liverpool in the first week of the New Year, I received a telephone call from London, to say that the Principal of the University College in Salisbury (later Harare) would like me to come out there for a week's visit! So, saying nothing to the members of the unit, and binding my secretary to silence, off I went – flying in a Comet aircraft with a stop in Khartoum. The Principal (Walter Adams, later Director of the London School of Economics) and his wife made me their house–guest at the beginning and end of my visit: the middle five days were spent up in Northern Rhodesia on a tight programme of visits. Apart from seeing the Governor, I met officials in the copper–mining industry; the (British) Director of African Education; and – most importantly – the leader of the movement for an independent Zambia, Kenneth Kaunda. I told him that if I came out to become the director of the Institute, it would be on the assumption of the country's independence, and then of the creation of a new university. of which the Institute would become the first element. On my return to Salisbury, I repeated this to the college committee dealing with the Institute. Somewhat to my surprise, I was still offered the job (with the rank of professor).

On my return home, I sat with Margaret and sought the way forward; we both felt it was right for us to go to Africa. So the next day, I went over to Manchester to break the news to the Vice–Chancellor, and to apologise for 'letting him down' over the chair in adult education. He was very generous and encouraging, and wished us well.

Looking back over eight years

I have never come across any convincing evidence to support the hypothesis of a 'male menopause', but I certainly found my 'forties' difficult and unsettling. My spiritual life was often anything but deep, and I found myself too often moved by impulse, rather than by the inward leadings of the Spirit. I certainly made many errors of judgment, and tended not to handle emotional relationships well. Although our family life was on the whole good and rewarding, and we had many holiday adventures, and lots of fun, I was probably too strict as the father of teen–age youngsters, which didn't enhance their self–confidence. I do not know whether this merely reflected my own insecurities at the time, or whether there was more of my own father's temperament in me than could have been wished.

In 1958 and again in 1960, Margaret experienced spells of menopause–related illness, but was very much herself again in good time for our 1963 African adventure. By then Keith was in the third of his four years at Trinity College, Dublin (where he read physics, played a lot of hockey, and greatly enjoyed Irish Quakers); Joy was about halfway through her five–years course at the University of Edinburgh, combining a degree with nursing studies – the first such course in Britain. She became a keen climber, at a time when there were few women involved in the sport, thus fulfilling a prophecy I had made one

Sunday morning at the top of Great Gable, in the western Lake District, when she was about seven years old: 'That girl is a born mountaineer!'. It was partly with that in mind that I had sent her in 1959 to the first Outward Bound course for girls, held in Devon – where she astonished a rather bored instructor (on loan from the Royal Marine Commandos) with her keenness and aptitude. It was fascinating to note the concordance of physical and other attributes, demanded by rock–climbing, with those associated with ballet dancing. She is still climbing most weekends nearly forty years later!

Keith and I built a two–seat decked kayak–type canoe; before its first use, I sent him on a training course so that he could teach me the basics. Joy picked up the same skills on her Outward Bound course. Over the years we had much fun, and a lot of spills! In 1962 Margaret and I took the canoe with us on a long holiday journey in Scandinavia, in our VW 'Devon' motor caravan. Starting from Copenhagen after attending an international conference on occupational psychology, we went *via* Stockholm; the night ferry across to Turku in Finland, thence to Helsinki. From there we drove due north right into Finnish Lapland, above the Arctic Circle, before turning west through the mountains into Norway, and south to Oslo before back–tracking to Bergen for our return voyage to Britain. For very many years we kept in touch with friends in all four countries, making visits when opportunity offered. When we left for Africa the canoe and its equipment continued in service with a Merseyside youth club.

The start of a new movement

Following the Merseyside industrial survey of attitudes to the older worker, I became convinced of the necessity for provision of preparation for retirement. The opportunity to do something about this came through a visit to Sir Alfred Owen, the managing director of a large group of manufacturing firms, with its headquarters in Darlaston, Staffordshire. He had opened a special workshop where some of the retired shop–floor workers could be employed on 'real work' part–time. He – and his daughter Grace, working in the personnel department – were enthusiastic and gave me their full support. I enlisted the willing aid of the local secretary of the Workers Educational Association, consulted with the relevant trades unions, and launched the first industry–based course in Britain of 'preparation for retirement'. The opportunity was

Rubery Owen Pre-retirement Course residential weekend: the first to involve wives

offered to all the men reaching the age of fifty during that year, and more than half availed themselves of the opportunity. Serving on a committee set up by the National Council of Voluntary Organisations, I prepared a short booklet, which was published under the title *Solving new problems*, in which I set out what ever after became known as 'Heron's six points' – the pre–requisites for a reasonably happy and fulfilling period of retirement. These were:

1. Good physical and emotional health.
2. Adequate income, substantially above subsistence level.
3. Suitable accommodation.
4. Congenial associates and neighbours.
5. One or more absorbing interests.
6. An adequate personal philosophy of life.

My emphasis was upon alerting people early enough to these needs, so that they could take such steps as were individually possible well before 'the axe fell'.

Just after we reached Africa in 1963, the Pre–Retirement Association of Great Britain and Northern Ireland was set up – of which more anon!

A Quaker concern

At Yearly Meeting in 1957 Anna Bidder, a Quaker zoologist from Cambridge, asked me and another Friend to meet with her during one of the lunch breaks. She told us that she had been approached by young Quaker students faced with homosexual difficulties, seeking help and guidance from Friends. She felt it laid upon her to join with others in addressing these matters. Later that year a group of Quakers with experience in biology, psychiatry, psychology, penology, marriage guidance, teaching and the law, began to meet regularly and did so for nearly six years. The group soon found that the study of homosexuality and its moral problems could not be divorced from a survey of the whole field of sexual activity.

Early in 1962, we came to realise that we were being called upon to publish our findings, and individual members began drafting agreed contributions for consideration. Every meeting of this group, over the whole period and including the preparation of a publication, was held as a silence–based meeting for worship. In February

Some members of the 'Towards a Quaker View of Sex' group

1963 a booklet was published under the title *Towards a Quaker view of sex*, I having served as editor. It aroused tremendous interest within and outwith the Religious Society of Friends, most of it positive and appreciative. Some inadvertent but important ambiguities were dealt with in a second edition, and the publication has remained in print, because of continuing demand, for thirty–five years so far.

Margaret subsequently was wont to say that we left Britain for Africa, four months after the publication of the booklet, 'because Britain had become too hot for Alastair'!

6 Field training

This may seem an odd title, but that it is appropriate will become clear later.

The journey out

In early June 1963 we left Britain for Africa, travelling by train and cross–Channel ferry from London to Stuttgart. There we met Joy and her university friend Mary, and took delivery of the Mercedes car that I had ordered some months before. Given the Quaker testimony to simplicity, this choice needs some words of explanation. During my short visit in January, and then on my return to Liverpool, I had made enquiries of many people with first–hand experience of driving in southern African countries. There was general agreement that sadly British–made cars at that time were simply too unreliable, and did not stand up to the demands of the terrain. My work would involve driving long distances on the few good main roads, followed by journeys into the bush on whatever roads or tracks there might be. The advice I received was to get either a French–made Peugeot or a German Mercedes. Given exemption from tax and duties, the costs were relatively low and differed little. So I plumped for the Mercedes, and have to put on record that it proved well–suited to the demands that my work imposed upon it, and never let me down.

We drove from Stuttgart, stopping overnight in Geneva, through the Alps to Genoa where we were to board the Union Castle ship that would take us through the Suez Canal and down the African coast to the port of Beira, in what was then Portuguese East Africa (later Mozambique), stopping en route at Mombasa and Dar–es–Salaam. It was a wonderful journey, and both of us appreciated the privilege greatly. Having driven up from Beira to Salisbury, where Walter Adams and his wife made us their guests, we soon pressed on northwards to Lusaka, and to the Institute where we were to make our new home.

It was located a few miles east of Lusaka, adjoining what was the *only* government secondary school for African boys in that colony. There was no equivalent school for girls, whose only chance was a place in one of the few secondary schools run by missions. The Institute consisted of a long narrow

central bungalow–type building, with
a full–length verandah, that contained
the offices and the library; a large
rambling house which served as a base
hostel for field workers; several small
brick houses for the European staff;
and a cluster of small brick–built huts
for the resident African staff and their
families. During my January visit I
had been dismayed to realise that were

Rhodes Livingstone Institute

we to come out to the Institute, there would be no alternative to our living in
a large two–story modern house (with a built–in self–contained flat for
visitors). This had been built with part of the funds allocated by the
Commonwealth Office for the re–furbishment of the Institute as a whole: I
never found out how my immediate predecessor managed to get away with
it. He had been a government anthropologist in East Africa, and was often
referred to as 'that bricks and mortar chap'.

On the day that we moved in, following the decorations and furnishing, we
found a feral cat had adopted us. We were told that it had been one of a large
number attached to the house of a woman anthropologist, and on her
departure been left to fend for themselves in the bush. We decided to feed
our adoptee, but to keep him out of the house. On one notable occasion,
Margaret heard him making a loud noise, so turned around just in time to
watch him 'seeing off' a spitting cobra successfully.

We were expected to employ several
African servants: by the expatriates
because that was the style to which
they had become accustomed; and by
the Africans themselves, because the
lucky ones would become regular
wage–earners, even though in a very
modest way. We gave a lot of thought
to this question, and in the end felt it
right to have two: one for the house,

Group of women from Margaret's 'sewing class'

one for the garden. The former was Joseph Mwanza, a young man who had only two years of primary education, but had managed to pick up a fair amount of English. In addition to the housework, he became a willing apprentice to Margaret in the kitchen: we never made him work in the evening (serving us at table!), and successfully encouraged him to

Unaccustomed Saturday afternoon exercise!

continue his education part–time at evening classes. He also enrolled as a part–time policeman. Joseph became rather like an adopted son to us, and until his eventual retirement from full–time police service (started when we left Zambia) we kept in touch with an exchange of letters once a year.

The new Director (Alastair Heron) of the Rhodes-Livingstone Institute also working physically one Saturday afternoon. [Unheard of by Zambian office and other staff. "Not done, old boy"]

Margaret was soon into her gardening, with great success, and later on was asked to teach practical gardening to women students at a new agricultural college nearby. At home, she formed a group of the wives of our drivers and other African staff, and on discovering that none of them knew how to sew, got them interested through the medium of patchwork pictures. She drew the outlines on the background cloth, and then showed and helped the women to sew on the patches of different colours. A year or so later, she had established a ready market for these down in the city, which enabled some of the women to earn a little money for themselves.

Getting to grips

Knowing in advance that the Institute was run down, but that funds were available for getting it going again, I took advice at the University College in Salisbury from one of my distinguished predecessors as Director, Clyde

Mitchell, who had taken psychology with his degree in social anthropology. Over the next two years I recruited research fellows in geography, economics, oral history and social anthropology, and also attracted others to come as research affiliates on funding they had obtained themselves. In 1965 I started the Human Development Research Unit, with three research fellows in psychology from the UK, one of whom (Robert Serpell) later became a Zambian citizen, married a Zambian, and eventually after various upheavals became my successor, first as director of what I had by then re–named the Institute for Social Research, and later as the holder of my chair in psychology in the new university. One of the others (Jan Deregowski) achieved an international reputation for his work on perception, first with Zambian children, and later on a wide cross–cultural basis. On his return to Britain he went to the University of Aberdeen, eventually (and in my view belatedly) being awarded a personal chair in psychology.

Once the British government had agreed to Northern Rhodesia becoming independent as Zambia, a provisional government was set up in Lusaka, but without responsibility for external affairs. On my arrival in late June 1963, I had of course immediately renewed contact with most of those whom I had met briefly in January. Kenneth Kaunda and

Independence Day celebrations

several of his colleagues welcomed my commitment to their new country, and to the creation of its university. I was appointed a member of the academic planning committee for the new university, and was involved in the project from its inception.

One of the most urgent aspects of the move to full independence was that of secondary education, for which there would be considerable funding. In April 1964 I was asked by the man soon to be the first Zambian Minister for Education to provide them with a secondary–school selection examination, that would be largely immune to charges of tribalism or regionalism, in a country with half–a–dozen major tribal groups. I explained that this could only be done by creating a mainly non–verbal instrument, rather like the 'eleven–plus' examination that we were abandoning in Britain. Zambia simply did not have the educated human resources to deal with anything other than 'objective' marking of the responses to 'either/or' and 'multiple–choice' questions.

This understood and agreed, I went ahead with the full–time help of an experienced schools inspector to prepare for a pilot run allowing just enough (of the four months available) to produce the final version and get it printed. This was achieved, and to ensure absolute fairness, packages of the examination papers were delivered **on the same day** to the principal of every primary school in the country, using government Land Rover vehicles and light aircraft. There were of course a few 'hiccups', but the operation was hailed as a complete success, repeated over many years with annually altered questions, and never made the basis of an accusation against the government of tribal bias. In 1965 I designed a civil service entrance examination along similar lines, intended to give intelligent Zambians who had not received a secondary education an opportunity. This is probably the point at which to provide the background to all this: at the time of Independence in October 1964, not more than 1500 Zambians had ever completed secondary education (regardless of result) during the whole sixty year period of British rule.

The effects of the Rhodesian UDI

Only a year after Zambian independence had been achieved, the government of Southern Rhodesia under Ian Smith decided on a 'unilateral declaration of independence' from Britain. The Labour government under Harold Wilson arranged for international sanctions on oil and other vital supplies, and promised full support to Zambia and to Malawi (formerly Nyasaland). A squadron of RAF fighter aircraft was stationed at Lusaka to dissuade Ian Smith from retaliatory action against the sanctions, using the Royal Rhodesian Air Force. In this connection, there was at the time a general belief that the RAF pilots would not in the event have taken effective action.

Zambia soon paid a heavy price for its full support of the sanctions, not only financially and in terms of oil and other shortages, but more subtly. Every weekend from Independence Day onwards, nearly every member of Kaunda's cabinet would be out of the capital, back in their home areas explaining the aims and plans of the Government to large gatherings of their people. This was an essential element in the major task of creating a nation from nearly fifty tribes, and from my frequent contacts with both ministers and permanent secretaries I had gained a clear impression that the policy was beginning to have the desired effects. But within a short time after the Rhodesian UDI, and the beginning of problems arising from the application of sanctions, most members of the Cabinet were needed either in the capital, or to go on missions abroad to enlist support and practical aid. At local level, not only did the campaign to increase national awareness wither away, but shortages of motor fuel began to erode the vigorous development programmes initiated since independence.

Making use of ignorance

I was given an unexpected opportunity to be in touch with government policy and some of the efforts made to implement it, when I was asked by the Minister of Agriculture to become the chairman of a new Agricultural Marketing Committee, to advise the Cabinet. My acceptance was announced in the National Assembly one afternoon, with the result that when I had walked the fifty yards or so from my office to the house, to have a break and a cup of tea, it was to be greeted by Margaret with 'I hear you've taken on another job!': she had been listening to the radio broadcasting the

Alastair with Tom Lambo, W.H.O. Director-General

Assembly session. She added 'The Minister said that the Government had asked you to do this, because it was certain of your complete independence; what he meant, of course, was that you didn't know anything about agriculture!' Right again. I chaired over fifty meetings of the committee, and travelled thousands of miles by light aircraft and by road, during the next three years. Despite the effects of UDI sanctions, the country was by then self–sufficient in maize, milk and other essential commodities. More significantly, the ex–Colonial large–scale producers were reasonably happy with the basis for market pricing mechanisms, and growing numbers of Zambian smallholders had been encouraged to move from a purely subsistence to a partial cash economy. And I had received a free education in sub–tropical food production and marketing.

University development

A Zambian zoologist (Lameck Goma) and I were the first two professors, working under a Canadian Vice–Chancellor (Douglas Anglin) and with an experienced Registrar from East Africa – an insomniac expatriate South African who 'lived for the job'. The University Council had decided to recruit staff on a fully international basis, with a good deal of success. Margaret and I made welcome the first 100 members of the academic staff (and wives), at evening 'get–to–know' parties involving a maximum of twelve people. I was able to design and equip proper teaching laboratories for psychology – the first in Africa south of the Sahara. The overall contract for the construction of the university buildings had been awarded to Yugoslav contractors, who employed their own site managers speaking a fair amount of English; local foremen also with varying degrees of competence in that language; and large numbers of locally–recruited Zambian labourers. It was far from surprising that there were many innocent misunderstandings, with resulting need to re–do sections of the work. I made a practice while the psychology units were under construction of making a daily site inspection along with the Yugoslav manager. One of

Kenneth Kaunda examines plans

the more difficult parts of one building was a 'floating room' for use mainly with work in auditory perception. I had explained that it was essential that there be absolutely **no contact** between the 'room' and the surrounding ground. I was away in the Copperbelt for a few days, returning only to find a solid concrete step leading up to the outer of the pair of doors forming the 'sound–lock'! They had to cut out a channel across the six–inch–deep concrete to break the physical contact as specified.

Behind 'the Iron Curtain'

Throughout the whole of 1965 and half of the following year, I had been working an average 80–hour week with few breaks, and was more than ready for our first leave. Early in 1966, the government of the Soviet Union advised the Zambian government that it had (unilaterally) 'twinned' our new university with that of Dushambe, in the Republic of Tajikistan. Shortly afterwards, we learned that a group, led by the Rector of Dushambe University, was about to visit us. Neither the Minister of Education nor the university authorities were very pleased by this high–handed initiative, but the Cabinet felt it politic to 'go along with' the scheme, since Zambia was in receipt of various forms of aid from the USSR.

As part of the University's reception for the Tajik visitors, Margaret and I held an evening party at our house in the Institute. Some of the visitors could manage a little conversation in English, but the Rector and his wife were dependent on the skilled services of their lady interpreter, a lecturer in their department of linguistics. At some point during the evening, I mentioned that Margaret and I would, during our forthcoming leave, be attending the International Congress of Psychology in Moscow. On hearing this, the Rector at once insisted that we return their visit by going on from Moscow to Dushambe, and undertook to make all the necessary arrangements.

And so it turned out – but of course not without difficulties! On arrival at the Congress in Moscow, we were approached by the Dushambe professor of psychology and one of his colleagues, who had been instructed by the Rector to bring us back with them, I was presented with a formal letter indicating that were being invited by the USSR Academy of Sciences to visit Dushambe, where the university would receive us as its guests. We had been booked on an Aeroflot flight, together with the two escorting academics. But during the week of the congress, a severe earthquake shook the area of Tashkent, only about an hour's flight from Dushambe – and all reservations to the area were cancelled. It came to the last morning, and we sat and watched all the hundreds of foreign participants in the congress depart for the airport. Finally there was nobody left but we four: and it was very obvious that the two academics were, quite simply, afraid to take any positive action – despite their obvious anxiety about the wrath of their Rector if we did not arrive. So I waited until the more friendly of the two ladies at the Aeroflot desk was on her own, and then went up and said quietly 'What do you advise, please?'. She glanced around, and then said 'Go out to the airport and try there'. So off we went, without the two academics.

Once there, I located the office of the Aeroflot manager, and presented myself to him. He was distinctly unwelcoming and at once said that there was nothing whatever that he could do: the only available flight was absolutely full. So I produced my official invitation from the President of the Academy of Sciences, explained that the Soviet Government had 'twinned' the two universities, and that this was therefore an official visit with a programme awaiting us. He read the invitation, and I then added 'I feel sure that we must avoid anything like a diplomatic incident over this'. While he took this in, I suggested that use might be made of the 'jump seats' ordinarily

The Rector of the University of Dushambe, (Tajikistan) with Alastair Heron on his official visit to Dushambe in 1966.

used by crew in transit. He then told me to join Margaret and our luggage in the departure lounge, and wait for him there, which I did. Not long afterwards, he returned accompanied by a stewardess and a luggage handler, and escorted us out to the aircraft. At the foot of the steps, he smiled and held out his hand, saying 'I am very pleased to have met you!' – which he clearly meant. So we went aboard and were seated, before all the other passengers came on board and filled the plane.

At the end of the 2000–miles flight, we stepped off the plane to be welcomed by the Rector and his wife, and a large group of university staff, including the lady interpreter whom we had met in Zambia. And so began a hectic four days, notable for the sheer friendliness of all but one of those whom we met. The exception was the local Communist Party commissar for education, who was not only formal and abrupt in his dealings with us, but publicly rude to our lady interpreter on more than one occasion. She explained to us privately that this Party man made a habit of creating difficulties for the university staff, and had the power to get away with so doing, through his influence on appointments and promotion.

The social highlight of our visit was a large–scale picnic on the banks of the river tumbling down from the Pamir Mountains. We all sat down around a 'table' of large Persian carpets laid on the ground, covered with an amazing assortment of what were locally regarded as delicacies' To us, some of them were: but all the various meats were only partially cooked! The hardest part was the necessity as the guests to take at least something from every dish, before it could be handed round the table to everyone else, We simply had to do our best on what amounted to a token basis! Before the meal, I had joined the Rector and some of the other men in a short swim in the ice–cold pale blue water of the river, which raised my status a bit, to judge by the smiles and general warmth of subsequent talk. The Tajiks are related to the people of Persia (now Iran), and at the time of our visit it was quite usual to see many women dressed in colourful silks during the evening. Although there was plenty of produce in the big marketplaces, the shops – even the main state department store – were characterised by empty shelves and few customers.

Disaster struck on the return journey to Moscow, when I found to my dismay that the Party commissar had failed to return our passports, that he had insisted on our handing over when we arrived. I was of course remiss myself, in that I had failed to remember them in the exuberance of our send–off by the university people. And so began a saga of delay and frustration, first in Moscow and then in Leningrad (now again St Petersburg), as a friendly official in the

Ministry of Health tried to re–unite us with our documents. Before going to Dushambe, I had been invited to the Ministry to hear their proposals for the provision of a Dean for our new Medical School. It did not take long for me to realise that they had no intention of letting their appointee go through our usual process of selection: the University of Zambia was simply going to get a Dean as part of the programme of unilateral aid to a developing country. So we spent

Driver; Guleva (interpreter); Margaret, professor of psychology at University of Dushambe 'outing', beside River Vakhsh (from Pamir Mountains) 1966

much of our time while waiting in Leningrad with this man and his wife, who were very kind and genuinely friendly, while manifestly scared of the authorities. He was a professor of dermatology, not a discipline that in those

days was given to producing deans for medical schools in Europe or North America, but in due course they were sent out to Lusaka. Not unexpectedly, he did not last very long as our dean, and I hate to think what happened to him on his return to the Soviet Union.

Eventually our passports were delivered to our hotel by a very

Tea garden in Dushambe (Tajikistan) 1966

arrogant young Party official, and we went off to the airport for the short flight to Helsinki. As the plane started moving along the tarmac for take–off, there was a collective sigh of relief, perceptible above the engine noise, and smiles all round: we were all getting out of the USSR. That's how it was in those mid–sixties years.

Our return journey to Zambia

I had ordered a new car for Margaret's use, a Triumph Herald station wagon model, and we had decided to drive it most of the way there, loaded with our extensive shopping (including a newly–available mini–bicycle for me). We went with it by air from Lympne in Kent to Basle; our land route was through western Austria into Yugoslavia, then north of Albania into Greece, down to Athens. The contrast in 'atmosphere' between Yugoslavia and the Soviet Union came as a welcome surprise. We found everything relatively relaxed, and were able to enjoy our visit to some Yugoslav psychologists and their families, and then a short stay in beautiful Dubrovnik. In Sarajevo we spent time in the Muslim markets, watching the metal–workers and sampling the Middle Eastern foods. Even allowing for the fact that we were just tourists passing through, we

Sarajevo market (1966)

noticed no signs of tension between the ethnic groups, and assumed that Tito and the (different) Yugoslav Communist system had achieved a united country from very diverse elements. Along with everyone else, we were tragically mistaken about this.

I had arranged for the car to be shipped from the Piraeus (the port of Athens) across to Alexandria, for transfer there to a ship heading for Mombasa, through the Suez Canal. But the Piraeus agents informed me that there would be a week's delay – because the small vessel involved had just been declared unseaworthy! I was assured that the one sailing the following week would be quite safe. So we took a short unplanned holiday in Crete, where there were hardly any tourists, and duly visited the Minoan site at Knossos. Having seen the car loaded at the Piraeus, we continued with our original itinerary, visiting Istanbul and Ankara before going on *via* Beirut to Cairo. There I was cheerfully provided by the Zambian Ambassador with a car and interpreter, to visit Alexandria and check that our car was being properly transhipped: much to my relief, I found all in order. While in Cairo we went out to the Pyramids, but had one great disappointment: the Museum of Antiquities was closed because of a state visit.

While waiting for the ship to reach Mombasa, we spent an idyllic week on the Indian Ocean coast south of the city, in a little cabin right on the shore, and sea–food meals at the parent hotel a few yards away. When the ship arrived and the car was unloaded safely, I had to spend several hours getting clearance from the Kenyan customs officer, who had if anything been too well trained by his British mentors! But eventually we got away and headed south for Dar–es–Salaam, and a short but happy time with our AFSC Quaker friend Lyle Tatum and his wife, plus a side trip to Zanzibar. Then we started the tough section of the return journey – down what had become known as 'the Hell Run', along which oil and other supplies were being shipped down to Zambia. Very often there was no sign of the road at all, except for the endless clouds of dust raised by the heavy trucks in both directions (they were bringing copper out for shipment at Dar–es–Salaam). It required quite a lot of driving experience and skill to safely pass the trucks, and I was thankful for

my FRS experience in Italy and of course also in Zambia itself. We reached the Institute at tea–time on the scheduled day, tired but 'triumphant' that Margaret's new car had come through such a varied journey unscathed.

Back on the job

During 1967 I spent a good deal of my time when not teaching, or otherwise involved in the work of the university, in preparing all the publications of the Institute for its change of name (to Institute of Social Research). For many years the Manchester University Press had published on behalf of the Rhodes–Livingstone Institute a series of full–length books; monographs under the general title of Rhodes–Livingstone Papers; and the Rhodes–Livingstone

Alastair Heron when Director of the Rhodes-Livingstone Institute, with former Directors Clyde Mitchell (l) and Max Gluckman (r), 1967. He brought the Institute (founded 1932) into the new University of Zambia as the Institute of Social Research.

Journal. Following tradition, I had as Director served as editor of all these publications. There had of course never been any possibility of the name 'Rhodes' being retained. 'Livingstone' on its own would have been acceptable, but was ruled out by the possible confusion with the Museum, located at Livingstone, near the Victoria Falls. So all the covers needed a new design, and my suggestion that we use the Zambian national colours of red, green and black was found acceptable. In the process, I added a new title – the ISR Bulletin – to provide an economical but attractive means of keeping the continuing evolution of the Institute before its 'public', both in Zambia and elsewhere.

I was also at last able to find time to initiate some psychological research of my own, with the aid of two part–time research assistants, one in the Copperbelt, the other at the Institute. The former was Marta Simonsson from Sweden, the latter Ruth Lockhart from Scotland, who had come with her husband Andrew on his appointment as a secondary school teacher, under the British developmental aid scheme. With their assistance I was able to develop a wholly non–verbal method of using one of Piaget's tests of cognitive development with Zambian children in the 7–12 age–range.

During the early months of 1968, it gradually became clear that Margaret was being afflicted by a recurrence of the 1958 and 1960 problems. This probably arose from a combination of two main causes: first, her progressive loss of an active role with the Zambian women, as these rightly became more independent as the country developed; and second, her increasing sense of need to be back with her own family, and with that of our son.

Margaret with her mother, sisters and Alastair's aunt in 1967

During our time in Zambia, we had been part of a small and changing group of Quakers and others interested, which met for worship in one or other of our houses, and also just socially on other occasions. So it was natural for us to join with two or three of them to seek a right way forward, and eventually it was clear that the time had come for us to return to Britain, at the end of the current university session in early December 1968.

The last job

During my last months I was asked by the Government to serve as a one–man commission of enquiry, into accidents in the mining industry. This followed upon a serious underground disaster at one of the mines in the Copperbelt. Given my normal duties during the week, this task had to be carried out almost wholly at weekends, sometimes with the Friday or Monday added. Quite often I was able to travel in a government or mining company light aircraft instead of driving the 200 miles each way.

The one man commission of enquiry prepares for take-off

The enquiry involved visiting every mine in the Copperbelt, plus one at Broken Hill, about 100 miles north of Lusaka. At each place, I made myself familiar with the whole site, above and below ground, and carried out interviews and held group meetings, at every level from the general manager down. My brief gave me full access to everything, including relevant records. The whole job took me four months.

When the time came to draft my report to the Minister of Mines, I had decided that it must be in two parts: the first mainly for the attention of the mining companies, and containing all the relevant detail, ended with recommendations for action aimed at the improvement of safety across the industry. The second part of the report would be shorter, and addressed to Government. Here I addressed the problem that I had identified when talking individually with the minority of underground chargehands and foremen who were Zambian. At that time, the process of Zambianisation underground was only partially complete, the majority of supervisory staff still being expatriate 'paleskins' from South Africa, Britain and elsewhere. I had found that the Zambian supervisors were faced with a two–fold problem, to which they had no workable solution. The miners over whom they were in charge had no experience of being given orders other than by expatriates, and tended to say 'Who do you think you are, giving me orders? Are we not all Zambians, all equal?'. But more seriously, some of the men complained to the local officials of the ruling Party, who then in turn went to the houses of the Zambian foremen, and threatened them and their families.

When I had the opportunity two years later to go up to the Copperbelt, during a visit to Zambia, I was very pleasantly surprised to be told that both the industry and the Government had acted on the recommendations, and that accident rates were already on a steady decrease. My 'commission of enquiry' had turned out to be a useful swan song.

The journey home

Having sold the Mercedes, we loaded Margaret's small station wagon 'to the gunwales', and set off southwards for Cape Town. Despite sadness at leaving Joseph and his family, and her women's group at the Institute, Margaret had progressively reached very good form as the prospect of getting back to England grew closer, which she retained all the way. Being overloaded, I kept the speed down, but we still had first a puncture, and then a blow–out – leaving us with no spare tyre. Luck was with us, though, for when we stopped for the night in the next town on our route, I found – right next door to the hotel – a garage which stocked the right size of tyre for our car!

We had never felt it right to take a holiday in the Republic of South Africa, though I had made one visit to Johannesburg, to the institute in which the director had offered me a job, back in 1954. When we arrived in Johannesburg, we called by prior arrangement at the Quaker office, and next day we were taken out to Soweto, where we were warmly welcomed. In discussion there was great interest in how things were working out in Zambia, which had been supportive of the ANC, and made an office available in Lusaka. In Cape Town, we were the guests of the widow of the former Vice–Chancellor of the University there, who had stood up for his staff and students against the government pressures. Then we boarded the Union Castle liner on which we sailed to Southampton, to be greeted at home by Margaret's family. A few days later, we went to Cambridge to join Keith, his wife and her two sons (her previous husband had died suddenly), and our grand–daughter.

Looking back

We both felt ourselves to have been privileged to spend upwards of five years in what might fairly be described as a key situation. Almost anything one did reasonably well was serviceable, and we valued both the general friendliness of ordinary Zambians everywhere, and the closer personal friendships we had been able to make. Until the University had recruited some staff, I was the only academic in the country, and Kenneth Kaunda and his colleagues had not hesitated to give me opportunities for service. It was both humbling and encouraging to know that our commitment to the new country was trusted completely.

Kenneth Kaunda is a remarkable man, with the ability in private conversation to make one feel that one has his undivided attention. We had of course been fortunate in getting to know him and his wife Betty, when they lived in an ordinary government house before independence. It was to that house, very early in the morning of Independence Day (24 October 1964) that Margaret delivered to them the tapestry she had made, depicting scenes in the life of the country, and which I had framed. They were delighted, and when Kenneth exclaimed that it would have a prominent place in his office at State House, Betty stepped in and claimed it for **her** office! When we celebrated our silver wedding in November 1965, they accepted our invitation to join us in a private meal at our house – but came 24 hours early! The next thing I knew was that Betty was helping Margaret in the kitchen, while a friend of ours escaped into the flat before we could stop her!

As time went by, I came more and more to the conviction that Zambia had been *unfortunate* in having the wealth arising from the copper mines. Not only did the Zambians in the Copperbelt aspire to incomes and life styles enjoyed by the expatriates they were replacing, but the government found it difficult to persuade the people generally to work hard within a cash economy. There was, for example, an occasion when local people refused employment harvesting on a successful cotton–growing project, preferring to drift to the capital where already there were many unemployed squatters. Kenneth Kaunda went himself to the project and tried to explain things to the crowd, but failed and – being an emotional man – was reduced to tears. But along with others, I had to learn that there were other factors involved. Zambia is a

Tapestry woven by Margaret Heron and framed by Alastair Heron, presented to Kenneth and Betty Kaunda early in the morning of Independence Day, 24 October 1964

landlocked country, with six borders, a thousand miles from the sea. Its inhabitants had never felt the external trading influences experienced by both West and East Africa. And to this must be added the factor of multiple endemic disease including malaria, bilharzia, and sickle–cell anaemia; one perceptive government colonial medical officer had once observed of Northern Rhodesia that 'it is a lucky African who suffers from only *one* endemic disease'. And finally, there was the almost complete lack of education, and the tribal and linguistic heterogeneity, to which reference has already been made.

Like many others, I came to love the people and the country, and gained from the experience. As a Quaker I tried to live on the basis that every human being is equal in *value* in the sight of God, however unequal they may be in human terms, and I didn't need to be a communist to believe in the merits of a classless society. So I was in a way prepared for the African attitude towards equality: but I had never seen it in action, or encountered a norm of consensus decision–making. One evening I was with a group of Zambians that included the Secretary to the cabinet, whom I knew well. 'Tell me, Dominic', I said, 'Why are there so many newspaper leaks of government decisions?'. 'Oh, that's easily explained. The discussion goes round and round in a seemingly circular fashion, but it is in fact a sort of spiral. Eventually consensus is reached – and somebody slips out of the room to leak it, before the process starts all over again!'. He added 'Of course I'm exaggerating a bit, but that 'spiral' process is what everyone is used to back in their villages'.

Later I realised that I had been through a sort of 'field training', that would affect the way in which I approached secular decision–making, and situations in which my position carried authority.

Alastair Heron with Kenneth Kaunda

Recent developments

Thirty years later Zambia is in deep trouble. Yes, Kenneth Kaunda made errors of judgment, and there was probably a critical period in which he became almost paranoid about some of his colleagues and civil servants. But there was corruption which he had been unable to stem, despite his deliberate policy from the outset of ensuring that ministers were well paid, and so could afford to behave properly. When the income from copper fell drastically, Zambia was unable to adjust quickly enough to the need for economic discipline, and started on the slippery slope of debt, and involvement with the World Bank and the IMF. As key services have been weakened, Zambia simultaneously has become one of the countries most afflicted by Aids. Government is visibly inefficient, and inflation has risen unchecked. Unable to make a personal visit, all that I can do is to help in a small way from a distance: one example will serve to put the situation in perspective. Recently I provided the funds for the purchase of a photocopier by the department of psychology at the university, to increase the availability of scarce teaching materials. The staff had agreed in saying that this 'would make all the difference in their work'.

7 As things turned out

During the months preceding our departure from Zambia, I had of course been applying for the few likely–looking academic jobs in Britain, and had my friends on the look–out for opportunities. It was a bad time to return, because the big expansion following the Robbins report on university provision was now over, and vacancies only arose when incumbents retired or moved elsewhere. In the event, I was short–listed and interviewed for only one chair, that of psychology in the first wave of appointments for the new Open University. Having identified the other main candidate, and being aware of his connections, I was unsurprised to learn that he had been appointed. But I was equally unsurprised to learn only two years later it had proved necessary to 'move him sideways' (since he had tenure to retirement age) and make a fresh appointment. Being a realist I had not confined my search to the university world, and was in fact interviewed for the job of General Secretary to the Marriage Guidance Council (subsequently called 'Relate'). In my view understandably and rightly, it went to the 'sitting' Assistant Secretary.

I was not short–listed for any of the three other chairs in psychology for which I had applied, despite my imposing array of referees: a serving Vice–Chancellor, a Fellow of the Royal Society, and the Director of a major foundation. There was of course an explanation, which reflected the academic culture of Britain. Although lip service was paid to periods of work abroad, these had to be of relatively short duration. The standard comment about anyone who had been abroad overlong was 'Of course, he's out of touch now'. A wholly inward–looking philosophy, it ignored everything with which the person concerned might have been 'in touch' abroad, and which might well be serviceable back in Britain. It tended to apply less in the 'hard' physical and biological sciences.

Off to Australia

Well before our decision to leave Zambia was taken, I had accepted an invitation to spend my 1969 leave as a visiting professor in the Australian National University at Canberra. So leaving a few further applications to take their course, we set off at the end of January, going by way of Barbados to visit close friends there, and New Zealand where a former member of the Liverpool team had settled with his family. On arrival in Canberra, we were provided with a university flat, and I bought second–hand a small Austin car for our use. We were very warmly welcomed, both in the Department, and by the members of the Quaker meeting in Canberra. Within a few weeks of our arrival, I was in receipt of what must be called a 'strongly–worded request' to visit Brisbane, and consider a firm invitation to accept a new chair in psychology at the University of Queensland. I was very aware of Margaret's hope that we would re–settle in Britain, and explained this carefully. They still pressed us to come without any prior commitment, so we agreed to do so, and were royally entertained. Although still without any sign of a job in Britain, I felt it right to decline the appointment, and carried on with my work in Canberra.

On collecting our mail on arrival in New Zealand, we had learned that our daughter Joy, who had gone straight from her graduation in Edinburgh to a nursing job in San Francisco, had decided to get married – to a well–known American climber – and settle in Boulder, Colorado. This news had contributed to Margaret's unsettled feelings in Canberra, and I was at a loss what best to do. Eventually she agreed to my suggestion that she go ahead of me to the USA, on our return journey to Britain. To break the journey, I arranged for her to stop over in San Francisco with Elizabeth Colson, a former director of the old Rhodes–Livingstone Institute, whom Margaret had met and liked. She would then see Margaret off to join Joy in Boulder. Only much later did I learn that Margaret found the whole experience very stressful, even though she was temporarily re–united with Joy.

Meanwhile, I gave up the university flat, and moved into a hall of residence along with other visiting fellows and professors. I started to think about my course of action if, as increasingly seemed likely, there was no job forthcoming back in Britain. Finally I decided to try in Canada, where I had several contacts, after I had rejoined Margaret: it was after all significantly nearer to Britain and our families than was Australia.

Out of the blue

During August, on the Tuesday evening of my last week in the Australian National University, I was called to the telephone. The caller was a professor in the psychology department of the University of Melbourne, where I had given some invited lectures a few months previously. The conversation went like this: 'Am I right in thinking that this is your last week at ANU, and that you will shortly be leaving Australia?' *'Yes, that is correct'.* 'May I seem rude to ask, but do you have a permanent appointment yet?'. *'No – I do not, so I'm proposing to join my wife in the States and then go up to Canada, where I have some contacts'.* 'Well, I'm breaking all the rules, but I think you ought to know that within the next two days you will be receiving an invitation to become head of our Department of Psychology. Some of us have worked very hard to bring this to fruition, and I hope to goodness that you will decide to accept'.

I was faced with a major decision – and Margaret was thousands of miles away. The situation was quite different from that in which we had no doubt about declining the Queensland offer; at that time, I still had some possibilities back in Britain. These had by now all come to nothing. But I was still keenly aware of Margaret's needs for the family and to be settled back in a familiar world. I sent her a cable, explaining the whole situation, and asked her how she felt about it. She replied briefly, to say that she was willing for me to go ahead and accept the Melbourne invitation. So I went down to meet the Vice–Chancellor, and to visit the department which was, incidentally, larger than any in Britain at that time. Having had a strong emphasis on social psychology through the interests and ability of the man I would be succeeding, the department was not well equipped with teaching and research laboratories, so I had to make the provision of these a condition of my acceptance, together with a couple of new lecturer posts. As I did not need to take up my position until the beginning of February, it was agreed that I should return to Britain and make a short tour around some of the more active departments there, to pick up useful ideas and methods. We were offered a choice of travel back to Australia, by sea or air, and chose sea – mainly to solve the baggage problem – and left the arrangements to the university and its agents in Britain. We had no idea that this would involve us in an event that justified a note in maritime history.

A 'floating typhoid time–bomb'

We sailed from Southampton on 16 December 1969, on a P&O ship called the *Oronsay,* of 28,000 tons and nearly twenty years old. We simply did not believe our eyes when the steward brought us to our first–class cabin: it belonged to a different era from what we had experienced in 1963 or 1968, on our journeys to and from southern Africa. It was small, the same size as a 'two up/two down' 4–berth cabin, but with only two bunks, and was without shower or toilet. The route to Australia was *via* Madeira, Florida, the Panama Canal, Acapulco, San Francisco, Vancouver, Hawaii, and New Zealand – a compromise between a 'liner' service and a 'round–the–world' voyage.

The Atlantic crossing was rough, and there many cases of influenza aboard, the result of one of the worst epidemics in Europe for a decade. Margaret was a victim, though fortunately not too seriously: I escaped with a lingering sore throat.

This is no place for a travelogue, so I will jump ahead to the evening after our departure from San Francisco (13 January), when the captain received confirmation that four members of the crew put ashore at San Francisco were suffering from typhoid fever. It was later revealed that this had turned out to be the case with others put ashore earlier, in Florida and at San Pedro, the port for Los Angeles. On arrival at Vancouver, the captain was instructed by the Port Authority to enter the harbour flying the 'QQ' flag ('My vessel is suspect: I need medical clearance'), and not to permit passengers or crew to disembark without medical clearance. Later the ship moved out to anchor in the harbour, about 200 metres from the dockside. The *Oronsay* stayed in Vancouver harbour for three weeks, with the majority of its 900 passengers and 500 crew aboard, while a team of epidemiologists and the Public Health Laboratories sought the typhoid 'carrier(s)'. The many and detailed inspections showed that the hygiene standards in the galleys and storage areas were extremely poor, and the origin of the outbreak was eventually attributed to an 'accident' involving a reserve water–tank, that took place while the ship was in port at Southampton. The typhoid 'carrier' almost certainly was one of the 40 crew members flown in from Goa (to join the existing 180 already on board).

During the enforced isolation out in the harbour, the entertainment staff of the ship did their utmost to 'keep up our spirits', and gladly accepted help in this from passengers. I ran a regular series of afternoon record concerts of classical music as a contribution to this effort. When it became obvious that communication between the captain (and a P&O director flown out from London) and the passengers had broken down, a meeting of passengers elected me as their representative at all discussions about the situation. The owners were very much on the defensive, and in fact there were some occasions when I had to combine firmness with the need to reduce tension. Midway through the second week, a plane load of passengers were flown to Australia and New Zealand, having passed a medical examination on the ship, and cleared to disembark. We did not seek to take advantage of this, partly because Margaret was still 'under the weather' physically and emotionally, and we felt the coming voyage through the Pacific would give her a chance to recover fully before reaching Melbourne. This we did, a month later than intended, and just in time for the start of the new session at the university.

A fresh challenge

We travelled overnight by sleeper on the train from Sydney to Melbourne, to be met at the station by Sam Hammond and his wife Marge (he it was who phoned me that evening in Canberra). They took us to their home near the university, and then to the very pleasant small furnished house in the inner suburb of Carlton, that the university had put at our disposal, until we could find and furnish a place of our own. Marge Hammond took Margaret under her wing, and did her utmost to help her settle into an unfamiliar situation. Meanwhile I was quickly immersed in meetings, both in the department and more widely in the university. I was greatly helped by the department's secretary whom I had 'inherited' from my predecessor, and Irene Kinsman and her husband became close friends, remaining in annual contact through the years.

Before leaving Britain, I had given much thought to my approach to the department of which I was to be head. I had been made aware of various personal tensions and individual difficulties, and felt it was important to address these squarely at the outset. On reflection, I decided to write ahead, inviting every member of the staff – teaching, secretarial, technical – to write to me in confidence about their hopes for the department and themselves. I also undertook to have a private meeting with every one of them as soon as possible after my arrival.

I found that quite a few had taken up the invitation to set out their feelings on paper, which was encouraging; and I managed to meet individually with all 35 staff members during the first three months.

There was a tradition of holding a monthly staff meeting, open to all, with the head of department in the chair. One day, after about four such meetings had routinely taken place, my secretary came in to say that some staff members would like a few words with me. Moving over to the chairs and coffee table at the end of my room, I made them welcome, and invited them to go ahead. After some

University building, Melbourne, showing Department on upper floors

hesitation, one of them said 'Well, Professor, we've been asked by quite a number of the staff to find out why you never put anything to the vote, to reach a decision'. As I certainly had no intention of turning the staff meeting into something resembling a Quaker meeting for business, I simply replied that it was my aim in the chair to get 'the sense of the meeting', and if possible to reach general agreement on the matter in hand. One of the others then asked if that meant I would never take a vote, to which I replied that if I did not feel general agreement had been achieved, I was quite ready to ask the meeting whether a vote was felt desirable. But I then added that if this showed that the meeting was very divided, I would prefer to defer the matter until the next meeting, to allow for informal discussion. The group expressed satisfaction with this explanation, so I undertook to put my proposals before the next meeting. This I did, and that is how decisions were reached thereafter: I recall only two or three occasions when a vote was taken, once with a clear 'split down the middle', another indicating a minority of disagreement. On that occasion I asked all those present to take note of the dissent, and to continue discussion informally outside the meeting.

Much later on, I think during my second year, I had another small delegation. This time it was to say that some staff members found it difficult to disagree with me in my dual capacity as department head and chairman of the staff meeting. That was easily solved, at least in part, by arranging for the election of a chairman and deputy, so that AH could 'sit in the body of the Kirk' and speak for himself. Of course there was no way in which I could shed wholly my 'persona' as head of department.

Student unrest reaches Australia

In those days it was noticeable that social movements originating in Europe or North America took about two years or so to affect Australia or New Zealand. To this the 'explosion' in the universities was no exception. So in 1971 we had a riot on the campus, and the doors of the Council Chamber were forced open when an emergency meeting was in session. The police were called and there was a determined 'sit–in'.

The next morning I was at work in my office when Irene Kinsman came through to say that a small group of people, including the chairman of the Professorial Board, would like to see me. So in came five people, to sit down around the coffee table. My professorial colleague explained that they formed the nucleus of what they hoped might be a constructive 'action group' – and they had come to ask if I would be willing to join them in this. I was genuinely astonished. One of the things that I had learned during my spell at the Australian National University was that newcomers from the UK – usually called 'Poms' or 'Pommies' – should 'keep their heads down', and strenuously avoid any appearance of wanting to 'throw their weight about'. This I had tried to do throughout my first year at Melbourne. So I said 'I've only been here a very short time, and I've got a lot to learn about Australia in general, and this university in particular!'. There was a silence, broken by the President of the Student Union saying 'Professor, perhaps you don't realise that what has been happening in the Psychology Department has not gone unnoticed; we think you have something to contribute in this crisis'. So I became an active member of what was soon called 'the Group of 11', which did in fact succeed in de–fusing the situation by setting in train a thorough review of the life and administration of the university, which at the time had about 12,000 students, in which I was very involved.

1971–73

Meanwhile the department made real progress, and some members who had long since ceased research found new interests. New staff appointments were made, including an additional professor, and I was happily successful in healing an inherited breach with the Medical Faculty. We were attracting students for honours degrees in greater numbers, as well as graduate students: this welcome development did however put a strain on our capacity for adequate supervision, one that was difficult to ease. I found myself able to continue the cross–cultural research that I had started in Zambia, and was one of the twelve founding members of the International Association for Cross–Cultural Psychology in 1972. In late 1973 I was elected vice–chairman of the Professorial Board, and *ex officio* one of the two Pro–Vice Chancellors.

At State House, visiting Betty and Kenneth Kaunda (1970)

It had come to seem that I was in the right place at the right time, for which I was profoundly thankful; but the same could not be said for Margaret. Within six weeks of our arrival, she experienced a major recurrence of her earlier difficulties. Following a period in hospital, she was put on a long–term course of drug treatment, the effect of which was to inhibit most initiatives. We managed to live a fairly normal life, and to visit other parts of Australia, going once to Papua New Guinea. In 1970 she accompanied me to Zambia, when we were the guests of the government on the occasion of my being honoured with the Order of Distinguished Service.

We had found a tiny 1900 detached house on a characteristic narrow plot (38 feet wide), in North Carlton, about 20 minutes walk from the university, in an area largely populated by Italian immigrant families. It had a minute garden down one side, with a lemon tree at the back and a fig tree near the

The Heron's house in North Carlton, Melbourne, with motor caravan (interior built by Alastair) 1974

front. On good advice, I had fitted an air conditioning unit to our bedroom so that there was somewhere to retreat in midsummer, when temperatures often reached 100F [38C]. There was just enough room, in the galvanised–iron garage at the back, for me to work on the conversion of a Commer van into a fully–fitted motor caravan. At that time, these were not available commercially in Australia, and it is just possible that I started what later became a movement in this direction. We greatly enjoyed a holiday in it, on the 'little island' of Tasmania. In many ways this is reminiscent of Scotland, with mountains and lakes, and highland trout streams, and I would happily have retired there had things turned out differently.

We were members of the Quaker Meeting in Melbourne, and also attended Australia Yearly Meeting, in Adelaide, Hobart, and Sydney. I served as clerk to elders, and in 1973–4 was joint editor of the Quaker journal *The Australian Friend*. Quakers in Australia, then as now, tend to be concentrated in the capital cities of the various states, with small meetings or worship groups elsewhere, It can be a spiritually lonely life, and the residential yearly meeting occasions are greatly valued by those who can get to them.

Mention has already been made of the Italian immigrants: the other succeeding waves were mainly from Yugoslavia, Greece and Turkey. The essential difference between all of these, and those coming from Britain, lay in commitment. The incoming families from southeast Europe often consisted of three generations; the extended family had 'burned their boats', and fully intended to become Australian citizens. This was often not the case with the British, coming out on assisted passages, who 'had a go', didn't settle, and went back to 'the old country'. This was the same pattern that I had observed in Montreal in the middle 1930s. It is obvious that we fitted neither pattern, and whether or not we stayed would be determined by personal factors.

In preparation for my first 'half–sabbatical' leave in 1973, I had to arrange for an academic situation where I could use the opportunity to get myself up–to–date with developments in my areas of interest. To give Margaret the maximum time with our families, I had to choose somewhere in Britain, and was fortunate to get a visiting professorship in Glasgow, at the University of Strathclyde. Well in advance of our departure, I had made arrangements for Margaret to see a leading specialist, whom I had known in my MRC days at Liverpool. I sent him an eight–page case history, covering her medical story from her early 20s. By the time I had finished drafting it, I had become convinced of the likelihood that her condition had been wrongly diagnosed, and I put forward a reasoned alternative. To cut a long story short, he eventually came to the same conclusion, and got in touch with my colleagues in Melbourne who were treating her. Fortunately, he was well–known to them, and respected. The upshot was that I returned to Melbourne alone, and Margaret joined our son's family in Cambridge. This was a welcome arrangement, coinciding with our granddaughter starting school, and Margaret's presence would enable Keith's wife to take a full–time teacher training course as a mature student. Margaret made good progress under the new treatment, and I found things going well when I 'commuted' from Australia to Britain for a Christmas/New Year holiday.

Staff of the Department of Psychology, University of Melbourne, 1974

The end of the road

During the afternoon of 3 April 1974, Keith phoned from Cambridge to say that Margaret was back in hospital. I left Melbourne the next morning on a 27–hour flight to London, having requested him to get in touch with her consultant (in Newcastle) asking if he could get to Cambridge to meet me – which he did. It turned out that he had asked a senior medical person at Addenbrooke's Hospital in Cambridge to arrange for some thyroid tests. This man, without getting in touch with him, had on his own initiative taken Margaret off the new medication that had been proving satisfactory: the outcome was catastrophic. I could of course have asked for an official enquiry, but quickly decided against it: I felt quite sure that Margaret's consultant would deal effectively with the delinquent. I accompanied her by ambulance to his department in Newcastle, where I left her in safe hands, and started my journey back to Melbourne. I had no doubt about what had to be done: explain the situation to the Vice–Chancellor, and resign my appointment.

I had plenty of time while in Britain in which to sit quietly, and try to be fully open to the leadings of the Holy Spirit. My faith in the love of God was rock solid, and I was willing for anything. My experience of 'being led' had often taken the form of becoming aware of what I called 'nudges' – thoughts coming into my mind unbidden, and without prior thought to generate them. On my way back to Cambridge from Newcastle, I suddenly thought of an evening in Sydney with a man I had known through my MRC work in earlier times. He had become the head of an internal Centre – for educational research and innovation – in the Organisation for Economic Cooperation and Development (OECD), in Paris. Might he come up with something, even on a temporary basis, for which my experience would be appropriate? I telephoned him, and he suggested that I arrange my return journey to provide a couple of days in Paris.

It turned out that they needed a consultant for a project in early childhood education, in which about a dozen of the member countries were interested. He was aware that I had for about a year been a member of an Australian Government working party on this very topic, and I was able to tell him that I was likely to be editing our report during the next few months, before I left Melbourne. He offered me a one–year appointment from the beginning of October, and I promised to let him have a decision quickly.

This is no place for false modesty: from the Vice–Chancellor downwards, my need to leave was greeted with dismay. Somehow or other, I had been enabled to win a place in the esteem of my colleagues far greater than I had realised: a Pom had made good quickly, and had been fully accepted. On the professional front, I was President–elect of the Australian Psychological Society, so I immediately put in my resignation to the Council, in order that a replacement might be sought without delay. But they refused to accept it, and my predecessor offered to serve for a second year, as my 'deputy'. I was encouraged to start thinking about the traditional 'Presidential Address', that they hoped I would return to deliver in 1975.

I felt it right to accept the Paris offer, and then simply got on with the full schedule of work – including the continued travel around Australia with the government working party. I was committed to presenting papers at two international congresses, to be held in eastern Canada in early August, so took the opportunity to travel *via* London. Margaret was back in Cambridge and getting on well, and relieved that soon I would be able to come over frequently from Paris for weekend visits.

On the occasion of conferring degrees at the University of Melbourne

In my last week at the university I was the guest at three dinners – the Faculty, the Students Representative Council, and my department! Having taken the chair at the Professorial Board for the last time, I was startled to find that everybody knew they had to stay on for a special 'tea', at which the Chancellor and the Vice–Chancellor made short speeches which succeeded in reducing me to tears in a very public way. Before leaving Melbourne, on the recommendation of the Vice–Chancellor I was made Professor Emeritus. My four years and seven months in Melbourne had proved to be among the most significant in my life until then. And I remembered again with gratitude my 'field training' in Africa: I am utterly convinced that the pre–Africa Alastair Heron would **not** have been 'the right man' for the Australian challenge.

The year in between

The headquarters of OECD in Paris are situated in Passy, near the Bois de Boulogne, and they had found me a third–floor studio apartment (one bedsitting room plus toilet and kitchenette) about twenty minutes walk away, down the Avenue Mozart. Two minutes away a weekly street market was held, running right round the block, so I could make my purchases and get them back in the apartment before setting off to work. Three mornings a week I maintained the habit of jogging that I had acquired in Canberra, though for the first time was forced to break the rule set by the ANU medical officer: 'Always run on grass, never on the road or pavement'. I set myself the discipline of cooking a proper meal roughly half the time, eating out alone or with colleagues on other evenings. As my little cooker lacked a grill, I tended to go for fish dishes, There was a baker just round the corner, so I never lacked for croissants or fresh bread. I brought Kenya coffee back from my weekend visits to Cambridge (it was cheaper there!). Everything else could be obtained in the mini–market located in the basement at OECD, where of course a variety of wines was available at slightly lower prices than elsewhere. On Sundays if the weather was fine I walked around central Paris, and sometimes went to the small Quaker meeting. Although I did make several visits to the Louvre, I never went up the Eiffel Tower – and will always regret my stupid failure to visit the Rodin gallery and garden. I found Paris an amazing experience: it seems never to sleep, there is a throbbing pulse even in the middle of the night.

Most of my work could be carried out in English, so although my French improved it never became fluent. My accent, though not that of the average educated Montreal–er, was of course far from Parisian – more like that in Belgium, but strikingly similar to Breton or Normand, which is where most of the original French settlers in Canada came from. My two closest colleagues were from Britain and Sweden, and we got on together famously. The principal difficulty was encountered in relation to formal meetings, where protocol held sway. Once I chaired quite easily a discussion meeting involving some of the official 'named representatives' of countries taking part in the early childhood project – and got thoroughly ticked off for having done so. One of my successes, however, was in arousing support for including 'child care' in the remit, thus producing a report title that referred to 'early childhood care and education'. This was important at the time, because in the UK, for example, nursery education came under the Ministry of Education, while day care for the under–fives was the responsibility of the Department of Social Service – and they could hardly be persuaded to talk to one another, let alone work out a joint policy.

My colleague Tom Schuller joined with Jarl Bengtsson and his wife in purchasing a farmhouse in a village in north Burgundy, about thirty kilometres east of Chablis. There was a great deal of work to be done to re–furbish the interior, and I often went down with them for the weekend to do some carpentry. Eventually they started referring to me as 'the non–financial partner'! We used to go out on the Saturday evening to a nearby restaurant, which at very reasonable prices compared with Paris, provided superb meals, which of course were accompanied by a good selection of wines from Burgundy and elsewhere. The only snag was the return journey to Paris in the Sunday afternoon traffic.

During my twelve months with OECD, journeys 'on mission' to member countries included a trip to Denmark, Sweden and Finland, another to Austria and Germany, and brief visits to Belgium and The Netherlands. It was quite an experience to see Vienna, thirty years after my visit with Morris Beckelman, restored and throbbing with life. My colleague and I included a visit to the Prater, the large amusement park on the edge of the Vienna woods. Strolling round the booths in the shadow of 'the Big Wheel', we came across one with a line of target rifles, so of course I was tempted. The task was unusual: to extinguish lighted candles (the size one uses on a birthday cake) by 'shooting them out'. I asked them to let me buy a few rounds to 'sight' a rifle using a bulls–eye target, and then had a go at the row of fifty small candles flickering in front of me. My old neglected skills did not desert me, and soon there was a small group of visitors peering round me as I proceeded along the line. As usual, the prize was of the teddy–bear variety, but the fun was in the doing!

Britain was certainly well behind many other countries in the provision of early childhood care and education, and remained so for the next twenty years. The first signs that real progress may at last be made appeared with the policy statements of the new British government during 1997.

The OECD is often quite rightly referred to as 'the rich countries club', and this is reinforced by the fact that by the early 1970s the USA, Canada, Australia, New Zealand and Japan had become members. Towards the end of my time with the organisation, I was able to arrange a mission journey that included official visits to Japan and New Zealand with a short spell of leave in Melbourne. This enabled me to attend the annual conference of the Australian Psychological Society, and to deliver my presidential address, as originally hoped. Entitled *Development, adaptation and change*, it provided the means to bring together in a coherent way most of the topics upon which I had carried out research over a period of nearly thirty years. But it also enabled me to offer a challenge to my fellow–psychologists, to ask them – even within the structures and work of the Society itself – to be ready for change. But I brought it to a close by quoting Cromwell's words to the elders of the Scottish Kirk: 'I beseech you, in the bowels of Christ, to consider the possibility that you may be wrong' – and ended with a postscript: 'I may be wrong' – which I meant. The address was well–received, and was published the following year.

I had of course been very aware that it would prove difficult to find a suitable opening in Britain, at the end of my time with OECD. So I had asked all my friends and former colleagues to be on the alert for me, so that no opportunity was missed. One day in July I had a letter from a friend and colleague in the MRC unit at the Maudsley, Jack Tizard. He had gone on to make a substantial contribution to the way in which those then called 'mentally handicapped people' were provided for, and had become a recognised authority in that field, nationally and internationally. He wanted to draw my attention to an advertisement about to appear. This was for someone to set up and direct a new unit, funded by the Department of Health and Social Security (DHSS), that would evaluate the provisions made, by the health authority and by the local social services, for mentally handicapped people in the city of Sheffield. Jack strongly urged me to apply, even though I had not worked in the field of mental handicap – and pointed out that evaluation of service delivery was something quite new, so methods would have to be devised.

I applied, in due course was short–listed, along with three other applicants, and went to Sheffield to meet the selection committee (on which Jack served as the DHSS adviser). They decided to offer me the job, and I accepted – to start on 1 October 1975, nine days before my sixtieth birthday. Years later, not long before his untimely death from cancer, I was sitting at home with Jack, and without warning said to him 'I have a lot to thank you for: I suppose you said to the DHSS people something like "Just bring Alastair Heron over from Paris, and see what you make of him." He leaned back, and let a broad smile spread across his face: I hadn't been far out.

Following family discussions in Cambridge, Margaret decided to stay there in her grandmother role for another year, to let Keith's wife finish her final year of teacher training. I would go into one of the university halls of residence in Sheffield.

My OECD report was published early in 1976. Later I was commissioned by the UNESCO International Institute of Educational Planning to prepare a handbook, published as *Planning early childhood care and education in developing countries*, which turned out to be a best-seller – though I lost a long battle with bureaucracy, failing to get it published in a Spanish translation for use in Latin America.

Overview

I gained much from this short exposure to life in part of the international civil service. I found, for example, how much more difficult it could be to work for one's own ideals – though I was never called upon to act against my principles. My untaxed salary did pose a problem, though: it was by my standards enormous. Facing up to this, I tried to live sensibly in Paris, and when travelling, accepting that this life–style was a temporary experience. Over the years that followed, I used my considerable savings to finance our visits to Joy and her family in Colorado, and some long–distance journeys that it seemed right to make. Some went to help a close friend and his wife (not in Britain) to buy their own house. The rest I suppose was used to support 'good causes'.

I valued this unexpected opportunity to learn how cultures other than my own went about the nurture of their young children. And despite the lack of regular worship and fellowship with my fellow–Quakers – perhaps because of it – my faith deepened, and I grew–up a little more. It was a good year.

8 Roots and fruits

The Evaluation Research Group

In my talks to middle–aged and older men and women, taking part in courses of preparation for retirement, I used to say 'It's not true that "old dogs can't learn new tricks" : research has shown that they **can** – but it takes them longer, and they have to be more motivated, than would have been the case when they were younger'. When I arrived in Sheffield in late 1975, I certainly had some new tricks to learn! My motivation was high, but I would not have 'extra time' in which to learn them.

Fortunately, those involved in the services for the mentally handicapped, that my future team would be evaluating, would expect me to make myself known to them and to familiarise myself with the activities for which they were responsible, or in which they were actively engaged. So I decided to allot the first nine months to this, and to appoint only a secretary for the time being. By the time research staff were in post, I should be able to know what I was talking about, and have some clear ideas on a research strategy. I think that this approach did in the event work out well.

We were to evaluate a 'development project', which had special funding approved in late 1971. The intention was to use Sheffield as a working model for the provision of a coordinated service for people with mental handicap, to be provided jointly by the local Health Authority and the city's Social Services. Most of the funding related to capital expenditure for the provision of hostels and workshop training centres – a familiar pattern, since central government always tends to limit commitments of an ongoing nature, such as salaries for new posts needed for the implementation of an innovative project.

My unit was enabled to appoint three research workers on three–year contracts: any extensions would have to be negotiated in the light of circumstances. Since I would be involved in several of our research projects myself, our total research strength was in fact nearly four. In the four years 1977–1980 we produced thirteen project reports, copies of which were provided first to those involved in the study, and then widely distributed both within Sheffield and nationally.

In early December 1980, when all the team had dispersed to other employment, I applied myself to the preparation of a 'final report of the Director', which was finished ready for dispatch to London on Christmas Eve. Cross–referenced to the 13 project reports, it was only fifty pages in length, but concluded with trenchant criticism, giving rise to four recommendations. To give the flavour of this, let me quote a few lines:

'The Development Project gave Sheffield a unique opportunity to provide itself seven to ten years later with one of the most integrated and operationally effective mental handicap services in the country …. . What has Sheffield done with that unique opportunity? The short answer is that it has "muffed it". It does not have an integrated mental handicap service, not even a reasonably well–coordinated one. Some parts of the overall service are operationally highly effective, but many are not. There are features of the Sheffield scene that are unique or nearly so …. but there are also frequent examples of successful innovations elsewhere which leave Sheffield slipping behind…'

My report ended by listing what was needed in the light of these conclusions:

Remedies

'The fundamental remedy is to adopt, and to work out practical ways of implementing, a philosophy of service to the mentally handicapped which will guide and inspire all future planning and decision–making. That philosophy was stated in the Feasibility Study Report, and is now re–quoted:

" …to enable the mentally handicapped person to live as much a part of the community as his/her disability will allow".

Since living permanently in a hostel is not "living as part of the community", the target must therefore be clearly recognised and accepted – as it has been and is increasingly being recognised elsewhere – to provide accommodation and the activities of daily life in ordinary housing, and – to the utmost extent possible – in public educational, recreational, social and employment settings. Progress towards such a target will require the development of an array of integrated services which are imaginatively matched to the full spectrum of need, from the very dependent profoundly handicapped person to those who have been enabled to live as wholly independent persons.

Given the acceptance of such a philosophy, the strategy and tactics must be hammered out from a starting point defined by the present realities of the situation in the Sheffield area. These realities do not need to be rehearsed in detail: the essential point is the necessity to re–think in a fundamental way the uses to which existing buildings could be put within the framework of the new philosophy; the ways in which staff resources could be re–deployed with increased job–satisfaction to those concerned; and the systems, management structures and mechanisms of coordination, all of which are just as open to change as are the minds of those responsible for them.'

My recommendations followed:

1. That the Department should encourage the health and local authorities in Sheffield jointly to consider in depth the findings of the Evaluation Research Group, together with those of the Development Team for the Mentally Handicapped, the Building Evaluation, and the Sheffield Case Register, in the light of the Department's 1980 review document, and with the aid of the 'Checklist of Standards' (Improving the quality of services for mentally handicapped people).

2. That the purpose of such joint consideration should be to produce, within twelve months, an agreed detailed plan for the more effective use of all available statutory and voluntary resources in the service of the mentally handicapped and their relatives in Sheffield, with a clearly–defined emphasis on progressive expansion of closely–coordinated community–based services.

3. That the target of such a plan should be explicitly to develop an array of integrated services which will enable every mentally handicapped person to live as much a part of the local community as his or her disability will allow.

4. That the Department should undertake to assist in the production and implementation of the new plan through the provision of advisors, and in any other ways at its disposal'.

In view of the way in which 'care in the community' (for both mentally ill and intellectually–disabled persons) often failed in practice, especially during the latter half of the Conservative government's eighteen years in office, I must note here that when speaking to or discussing the third of those four recommendations, I always pointed out that 'this was not "a cheap option" – and would in fact probably demand **higher** funding to be successful'.

This report of our work as a team was accepted by the Health Authority and by the Social Services Committee of the City Council – and 'received with appreciation' by the DHSS department in London. The recommendations were implemented quickly, by the setting–up of a joint working party (including myself in an honorary capacity, since by then I had retired), which succeeded in producing a detailed report within about six months. Over the next few years, slow progress was made, with the Health authority making most of the running, until momentum was lost as the Social Services Department increasingly found difficulty in taking its full share. This was partly due to lack of financial resources, partly to difficulty in identifying suitable officers to carry out the necessary work. Much of the progress achieved was due to the efforts of my friend and fellow–Quaker Mary Myers, in her capacity as Consultant Psychiatrist (Mental Handicap). She was also co–author with me of the book *Intellectual disability: the battle against handicap*, in which the work of the Evaluation Research Group was made generally available. I made a tactical error over that title, because many potential purchasers of the book failed to realise that it was about 'mental handicap'. I was marginally ahead of the times: within a very few years the term in common use became 'persons with learning difficulties'. Our book title was derived from terminology reached by the World Health Organisation: a condition present at birth is an 'impairment'; the consequences, in terms of performance (physical, cognitive, emotional or in combination) are referred to as 'disabilities'; and 'handicaps' arise from the negative ways in which a particular society or culture responds to those 'disabilities'.

I spent the first three months of my conventional retirement on a visit to Australia and New Zealand, of which about half was as a guest in my old department at the University of Melbourne. That gave me plenty of time in which to feel my way forward in a new stage of my life when I returned.

Putting down roots

When Margaret joined me in Sheffield in the latter part of 1976, we set up house on a temporary basis as tenants of our friends Eric and Rosalind

Priestman, who had left Sheffield to serve as the Wardens of Woodbrooke College, the Quaker element in the Selly Oak Colleges in Birmingham. We had known one another in Friends Relief Service days, and Rosalind was the sister of my team–mate Enid, in northwest Germany. From this congenial base, we started the search for a house of our own. We looked at a few, and then one evening went to see a fairly large bungalow, near the southern edge of Sheffield, within sight of the Derbyshire moors. In minutes, we both had the feeling that this was the right one for us, and told the owners that we would go ahead the next day. Soon afterwards the agent reported to them and to us that they had received a higher offer. When we saw the owners again, they told us that they had 'turned down the higher offer because we wanted you to have our house'.

So on a brilliant cold sunny day at the beginning of February 1977, we moved in and started the process of turning a house into a home. Margaret was delighted to have a good garden again – and I felt ready to make a beginning! I had no gardening knowledge or experience, so I asked her if she would take me on as her apprentice. Perhaps wisely, she wasn't keen on that, so I just made up my mind to learn from books, but to ask her questions about the practical side. We readily agreed on a division of labour: she would concentrate on flowers and vegetables, while I would develop the shrubs and trees, and – later – the fruit. We inherited two sizeable artificial ponds, one above the other and intended to be linked by a waterfall. I struggled with these for several years, until fortunately an over–enthusiastic visitor put her foot through the liner of the lower pond: I cheerfully let it 'return to nature', complete with its annual show of yellow iris. In due course I had about a dozen fish thriving, keeping good company with newts, and invaded annually by the frog–spawning season.

When I arrived alone in Sheffield in 1975, I naturally started attending the Quaker meeting down in the city centre. For the reader unfamiliar with Quaker ways, let me explain that traditionally worship is based on what they call 'silent waiting upon God'. Anyone who feels moved to rise and speak is free to do so, thus contributing to the 'spoken ministry'. I was of course accustomed to this, and familiar with the need for self–discipline, for being very certain that it was right to speak, and also that it was the right time to do so. But it came as somewhat of a surprise to me, that during my first year in Sheffield I did not feel called to speak during meeting. This was a new experience, and I simply accepted it as an essential part of my 'inward training'.

Citizen advocacy

Immediately following the report of the Working Party on services for mentally–handicapped people in Sheffield, set up to respond to my final report from the Evaluation Research Group, I joined forces (as Chairman of a small representative committee)) with the secretary of the local Community Health Council to address a recommendation concerning the provision of a voluntary service of 'advocacy'. Unlike the only existing UK service of that kind, which operated inside two large mental handicap institutions in the London area, we aimed from the start at a service that would provide trained volunteer advocates, on an individual basis, to mentally handicapped persons, whether still at home, in a social services hostel, or living 'in the community' in ordinary housing. It was clearly going to be a long haul to obtain the necessary funding, but we succeeded in the end, and Sheffield now has a well–established service. That however does not mean that it is ever wholly free from financial uncertainties: the sources of funding, such as the City Council, are themselves vulnerable.

Pre–Retirement education

During 1976 I renewed my contact with the Pre–Retirement Association, and in 1978 was asked to serve as its chairman. Fifteen years after its creation, the PRA was still struggling financially, and in fact was only surviving through income earned by the provision of courses to a few commercial and industrial firms. These courses had become narrowly oriented to the financial aspects of retirement, and there had been an ominous shift from preparation to planning. Although usually based on my original 'six points', the approach was very much in the hands of the particular organiser, in the absence of an agreed syllabus. I soon realised that the future would depend on success in obtaining recognition and financial support from government.

This was very much a matter of 'easier said than done', not least because there was a marked tendency for the relevant ministries to 'pass the buck'. But I had no doubt in my mind that we should be dealing with the Ministry of

Executive of the Pre-Retirement Association (1985)

Education, making a convincing case that we were a potential provider of a special form or aspect of adult continuing education. This meant increasing the personal involvement of educationists in the structure and activities of the PRA, while not alienating those who were bringing in its funding from the commercial courses. The breakthrough came with the decision by the Ministry of Education to name a representative to us, who would serve on our Executive Committee. It was a long hard road to follow, but in the end we were successful, and the PRA was officially recognised as the 'focus' organisation, with an annual grant (in three–year terms) from the Ministry.

Here I should note the difficulty encountered by course organisers and tutors with the last of my 'six points', quoted earlier. They could cope, with or without specialist help, with such topics as health and finance, but usually not with 'an adequate personal philosophy of life'. Quite often, that topic was simply omitted from the syllabus. When I was thinking through the likely 'needs' back in the late 1950s, I soon saw that one might make a thorough job of preparing oneself in most of the practical ways, and still be unable to make a successful adjustment to a very different way of life in retirement. But I was not prepared to assert a need for a spiritual basis, let alone a religious one, even though that was what I believed myself. Hence the phrase 'an adequate personal philosophy of life', which offered flexibility while still affirming the need. I still think it is essential to address it.

My own 'retirements'

Looking back, I think of my departure from Melbourne in late 1975 as a 'first retirement', since it brought to an end my active career as a psychologist. Five years later, I reached 'pensionable age' and ceased full–time employment. The next five years were spent in a combination of voluntary activities, such as citizen advocacy and the PRA, with consulting and advisory roles. The latter included work for the Welsh Office, laying foundations for the development of service evaluation in the mental handicap field; preparing a report for UNESCO on the provision of early childhood care and education in Jamaica; and work as a consultant in that field for the World Health Organisation (WHO). During the same period I was also a governor of a residential school in north Wales, where pioneering work was initiated and developed by its principal, Martin Weinberg. Yes – it could be said that the end of full–time paid employment simply gave way to nearly full–time voluntary work, which I greatly enjoyed,

In February 1985 I spent three weeks as a 'sojourner' at Pendle Hill, a residential Quaker centre, just outside Philadelphia. One bleak afternoon, feeling the need to take the air after a long spell in the library, I went for a stroll round the small campus, Suddenly, words came into my mind: 'Go home and clear the decks'. That was all. There was no indication of 'why' or 'what for', so I resolved to await further guidance. I noticed then and later that when I mentioned this experience to various people, they thought the last word was 'desk'. In naval parlance the order 'clear the decks' meant 'in readiness for action'. So I came to see the need for taking one step at a time, not concerning myself with what might follow later.

Back home again, I gradually understood that I should begin a process of withdrawal from major ongoing commitments. I felt it important to do this in such a way as not suddenly to burden others, or cause organisational difficulties. For example, I gave the PRA a year's notice that I would be standing down as Chairman, and ensured that my successor would be able to move in smoothly. By the end of 1986 I had effectively retired for the third time – but found myself by no means idle. It became increasingly apparent that 'clearing the decks' was necessary, to release me for a period of 'active service' among my fellow Quakers locally, nationally and overseas.

'Travel broadens the mind'

This personal story would certainly be incomplete without at least summary reference to the many trips that Margaret and I made together. In addition to the ten visits she made (alone or with me) to stay with Joy and her family in Colorado (the last in 1986), we made two trips through France to Switzerland (there visiting our friends Pierre Dasen and Ashe Singh Williams and their families – the former the professor of cross–cultural psychology at the university of Geneva (and a co–founder with me of the International Association of Cross–cultural Psychology), the latter on the staff of the World Health Organization (WHO). On one of these trips we swung west to southern Brittany (and spent three nights in Balzac's house!).

Margaret and I travelled through France to Switzerland, in the mid-80s, visiting friends in Austria en route

In 1982 we drove through central Portugal from the north, as far as Lisbon and Estoril, where we stayed with Americo de Sousa, whom I had met when we both lived in the annex of a hall of residence in Sheffield, in 1975–76. A school teacher (but with an Oxford DPhil. degree), he has published several successful novels in Portuguese – unfortunately not translated into English, and so with a very limited market. When Margaret felt that she had come to the end of her trans–Atlantic flying, I decided on a programme of what for both of us would be first–time visits, each year shortening the journey for her. So in 1988 we went to southern Morocco; in 1989 to Sicily; Spain in 1990; and Guernsey in 1991. This was an enriching series for us, and rounded off Margaret's holiday travel as she approached her seventieth year. She used to refer to me as her personal courier!

A 'bricks and mortar' man?

In January 1987 I became clerk of the committee responsible for the use and maintenance of our Quaker Meeting House in central Sheffield. This coincided with an approach from a large firm of property developers, which was drawing up a plan for a radical re–development of the city centre. This would involve the firm in the purchase of buildings occupying the selected area, and our meeting house was one of these. This came as a shock to many members of the meeting, since the building had only been completed in 1964, as a belated replacement to the meeting house that had been destroyed in the Blitz. It was agreed, however, that a small group should meet with the agents for the developers, without commitment.

Members of the Sheffield New Meeting House Committee with the architects and quantity surveyor

Eventually, the meeting was faced with a decision: to agree in principle to the sale of the building on terms to be negotiated; or to sit tight and hope that the developers would fail to obtain a compulsory order. We decided to enter into negotiations, but on the clear and explicit understanding that a sale would only be possible if an acceptable freehold site elsewhere was identified. Here I must explain that the freehold of our existing site was exceptional in the city centre, and sites held by the city council were made available only on a leasehold basis. Our Quaker meeting set up a New Meeting House Committee, of which I was appointed convenor. When three of us, together with our solicitor, met with the agent and a director of the development firm, I started off by explaining that it was not our way to haggle, and that we tried to let our 'Yes' mean 'Yes', and our 'No' mean 'No'.

I proposed that a valuation of the present building and site be carried out, at their expense but by a valuer of our choosing. This was agreed. At a later stage in the negotiations, we agreed to a second valuation being carried out by a firm of their choosing: this left the situation unaltered. Great care having been taken to keep all our members fully informed through a series of discussion meetings, the decision was reached to accept an offer based on the independent valuations, and subject to the identification of a suitable freehold site within the central city area. A Quaker architect (Michael Sykes) was appointed, and a special meeting was arranged for all our members and interested attenders, at which he sat with his notebook recording the many and varied ideas for the new meeting house that were put forward.

One day, I arranged with an officer in the planning department of the City Council to go through the list of possible sites. There seemed to be three that merited inspection, so I went off and had a look, which quickly brought it down to one. This was a 'bomb' site about 100 metres from the Cathedral porch, right in the heart of the city. It presented design problems, but if these could be solved, offered great promise. Michael Sykes and his partner took up the challenge, and succeeded brilliantly. So we went ahead, and left our New Meeting House Committee to work through all the details with the architects, quantity surveyor and solicitor.

There were nine of us, and it was a wonderful team! During the last few months most members served as convenors of the small groups that I set up to work on the furnishing and equipment of the new building. I served on two of these, one for the curtains and the other for all the seating. For the latter, we obtained sample chairs from a well–known manufacturer of church seating. As Quakers are accustomed to sit in the meeting for worship for about an hour, without getting up, it was important to put any proposed chair to the test. So I asked two men and two women, one of each pair taller than the other, to serve as a test panel. We soon eliminated two models as unsuitable, and concentrated on the third. This seemed to require a small modification, so our architect arranged for a representative of the suppliers to meet with him at my house one evening. With the aid of my tool–box, he moved a couple of screws to meet my proposed alteration, and left the chair to be re–tested. It passed all four members of the panel, so we placed our order. I am delighted to record that we have never heard a word of complaint, either from our own people, or from the many groups that make use of the building. The first meeting for worship in the new building took place on 21 October 1990.

Quaker activity

From 1982 to 1988 I was a member of Meeting for Sufferings, the representative body that acts for the Yearly Meeting during the rest of the year. During the same period, I was clerk to a curious body called the Yearly Meeting Elders Executive. Its principal function was to identify a speaker for the Elders Meeting at each annual gathering of Quakers in Britain: it had no official status, but its clerk was a member *ex officio* of the YM Agenda Committee. So I also served on that for those six years, and what a great experience it was! Although it usually met only twice a year, the depth of fellowship was palpable, and I was quite sad when the time arrived for me to come off it. I have never seen service on any of the Society's departmental central committees, or on those concerned with ecumenical or with international Quaker relationships.

Half overlapping with that six years, I served as a Monthly Meeting representative on the Representative Council of Quaker Home Service, one of the three 'central departments' of the Yearly Meeting. I enjoyed and valued this experience, though often regretting that the Council had only an advisory role, not even contributing to the nomination process for appointments to the central committee of the department.

'Travel in the ministry'

As a church without a paid ministry, the Quaker movement became familiar right from the start in the late 17th century with the concept of 'travel in the ministry'. An individual Friend might become aware of an inward 'call' to visit other Quaker meetings in her or his own country, or to do so overseas. Sometimes they travelled alone, but quite often in pairs either with equal experience, or a younger Friend with an older one. During my time as a Quaker this practice has until recently tended to fall into relative disuse.

To Australia – Early in 1987, however, I became aware of such a call – to spend time in that way among Quakers in Australia. Having ascertained that such a visit would be welcomed there, I checked the religious validity of my concern with my local Monthly Meeting, which then provided me with a 'travelling minute'.

Residential Quaker conference North Queensland, at the beginning of Alastair's travel in the ministry for nine weeks in 1987

Beverley Worship Group, W. Australia, the last place Alastair visited during his travel in the ministry

It was arranged that I should prepare an essay, which would be published simultaneously with my arrival in Australia, and used as the basis for discussion with the various meetings and groups that I would be visiting. The itinerary, drawn up in Australia, started my journey in northern Queensland, and then took me right round through Sydney, Canberra, Melbourne, and Adelaide to

Perth in Western Australia. In addition to a side trip to Tasmania, other visits were arranged with small and isolated groups. The circuit took nine weeks. Later it was made clear to me that my visits had been well–received and generally helpful, perhaps especially to the small isolated groups. The essay was published under the title *Charity, liberty, unity: a Quaker search for essentials*, which was subsequently twice reprinted, mainly for sale in Britain. Each meeting and worship group had been given the choice between having me deliver an address based on the essay, followed by discussion, or everybody reading the essay in advance, so that all their time with me could be devoted to discussion.

On the way out to Australia, I spent a week in Japan, mostly in Hiroshima and a nearby large city. The purpose was to return the visit of a Japanese social worker, who had come to Sheffield some years previously to talk about the evaluation study. In Hiroshima I was made welcome and guided around by a colleague of his. She was the daughter of one of the survivors in 1945, so I was privileged to get so close as that to the realities of that terrible day. Although of course the city had been completely rebuilt, I found the visit very moving. On the last night of my stay I was the guest of my Japanese colleague and his wife, in their small house, and enjoyed being introduced to the domestic scene. I

Hiroshima Peace Garden

cannot claim to have slept well on the thin mat laid on the floor!

And to Canada – In 1989 I made a similar journey, spending nine weeks in Canada, coast to coast from Halifax to Vancouver Island. Canadian Friends had consulted with Australia, and produced a similar timetable. It was in fact too tightly packed, and I longed to have been able to stay longer in several places where ministry was clearly much needed. Canadian YM followed the Australian pattern, publishing on the day of my arrival in Halifax an essay entitled *Speaking to our condition: a ministry to Friends*, and giving groups the choice over its use. (This too was reprinted more than once, again mainly for sale in Britain).

First meeting (in Halifax N.S.) of Canadian 'travel in the ministry' (1989)

In one of the prairie Provinces, there were only a few Quakers, so they arranged among themselves to have a day with me. This they did by hiring a room in a pensioners club in a small town, upon which we converged from north and south, each group covering about 150 miles. Seven were there, plus a couple of Attenders – and it was a good get–together. The value of such travelling ministry is attested by their minute, which read:

'Alastair Heron's visit with Prairie Monthly Meeting, though short, has provided the catalyst for a renewed commitment to spiritual growth amongst our members. We are indebted for the opportunity to hear Alastair's ministry, and consider its relevance to our own situation. His willingness to travel a great distance to share his convictions in unknown situations, and with people he had not met, has helped us to realize the need to share more freely among ourselves, and to reconsider the importance of the spiritual life of our meeting.'

Alastair with Catherine Molnar at the western end (1989)

On Vancouver Island, I was much attracted by the city of Victoria, which has a definite character of its own – much smaller, of course, than Vancouver with its panoramic setting, which I was glad to visit under more favourable circumstances than in early 1970. On the Island, in addition to the meeting in Victoria, I stayed overnight near Nanaimo to enjoy a shared lunch with the small Up–Island

Worship Group, and had a good discussion. My hostess Catherine Molner was a Scot, born in Perth, trained as a nurse in Edinburgh, and subsequently worked in Sheffield: I could hardly have made a better match than that!

Woodbrooke – and the surveys

In the autumn term of 1988, and again in the spring term of 1990, I was a 'Friend in residence' at Woodbrooke College, the first of the Selly Oak Colleges in Birmingham, founded in 1903. During my term in 1988, I found myself wrestling with a growing concern about the 'health' of the Quaker movement in Britain – if, in fact, it could be so described. The membership figures had levelled off at about eighteen thousand or a little less, but this was in sharp contrast to the steady increase in the number of those who attended a Quaker meeting fairly regularly, often for many years, but of whom extremely few applied for membership. I set out my thoughts in a brief paper which I distributed to colleagues, and asked for a meeting close to the end of term. The object was to seek 'clearness', to see whether or not I was experiencing what Quakers call a 'concern' – a sense that God is laying a task upon one, a call that one should not evade. The clearness meeting did feel that this was the case for me, and the suggestion was made that a small support group be formed, to help me in the process of finding the way forward. This met several times during 1989.

In the outcome, it was decided that I should carry out a survey of the views and experiences of attenders, across the whole of Yorkshire, The main object was to provide them with an opportunity to speak for themselves: it was usually a case of some member expressing an opinion on their behalf: 'Attenders feel that … etc'.

I hoped that the survey 'would yield clear indications of ways in which they might be better informed, nurtured and encouraged'. During 1990, I designed a two–stage survey, the first consisting of a postal enquiry, the second of individual interviews. Nearly eight hundred listed attenders in the forty Quaker meetings in Yorkshire received a copy of the schedule of questions: sixty per cent responded. One hundred and seventy–five of them indicated a wish for a personal interview. I made up a fifty per cent sample of these, stratified for age, gender, location and size of their local meeting, and managed to meet with seventy. These interviews made necessary about 1500 miles of driving, spread over eight weekends in late 1991.

Full details of the results obtained were published in 1992, under the title *Caring – conviction – commitment: dilemmas of Quaker membership today*, so there is no need to inflict the details on present readers. I hope that it will suffice to quote the four principal findings;

—*many attenders keep on coming to a Quaker meeting because they find there a place of acceptance, of caring, of support. For an unknown number of them, it constitutes a 'safe haven', perhaps their only one. Significantly more of them come for that reason, than for the opportunity to worship or meditate.*

— *nearly forty per cent felt that 'there is no need to make a formal commitment through membership'.*

— *the main criticism was about the inaccessibility of the information that an attender might welcome or need.*

— *Quakers were seen as poor communicators, at a personal face–to–face level. On matters of faith and experience, they tend to be diffident, and to be seekers rather than finders.*

Quite a number of people suggested that it would be useful to seek the views of those who had recently become members. So I went ahead and approached all those (throughout Britain this time) who became members of the Society in the year 1992. Two hundred replied to the enquiry, once again a sixty per cent response. The results were published in 1994 under the title *Now we are Quakers: the experience and views of new members*. The first finding was that more than half these new members had reached fifty years of age, and the ratio of women to men was above three to two. Nearly half reported receiving no encouragement to apply for membership; more than one in three a lack of nurture since becoming a member. And as many as two out of three reported 'very little' or no interest in the 'central work' of the Society: hard evidence of parochial or congregational attitudes.

It gave me no satisfaction to have shown conclusively why our 'recruitment rate', from our nine thousand recognised attenders, was as low as four per cent a year. But I think that I may have made some contribution to a remedy, by responding to the clear call from attenders for a handy source of information about the host of acronyms, and peculiarly Quaker terms, with which they were confronted. This was a pocket–sized booklet called *QuakerSpeak: first aid for newcomers*, that 'unpacked' 60 acronyms, and provided concise definitions of more than 150 Quaker terms. A thousand copies of this were sold in three years, justifying a revised second edition. By the way: like most Quaker authors published by or on behalf of the Society, I received no payment, so it might be called a labour of love!

Quakers in Britain

Early in that same year (1994) I came to feel a strong call to study the changes that had taken place among Quakers in Britain, at least during the fifty years of my own membership. From that it was but a short step to making that a century – from an event in 1895 known as 'The Manchester Conference', the centenary of which we were approaching. This was a week–long gathering of Quakers from all over Britain, numbering about 1500, to hear papers and to discuss the issues raised by the then–recent advances in Biblical criticism, and in scientific matters, notably the theory of evolution. Though opinions vary, this could well be seen as a key moment in Quaker history.

Knowing that a 'Summer Gathering' was planned for mid–August 1995, to be held at the University of Lancaster, at which hundreds of Quakers and attenders would be present, I made that my target for publication, and planned my work accordingly. But the unforeseen happened: as described below, a badly–infected foot saw me in hospital for a total of six weeks in August and September 1974, so I was unable to start work until the end of October. My friend David Woolgrove, who had agreed to publish the proposed book, provided me with a deadline for the main body of the script – Easter 1995 – that would guarantee publication at the Summer Gathering. That gave me six months, roughly two months for the library research, and four months for the actual writing. This turned out as seven overnight visits to Woodbrooke College, for the library work (the library is uniquely open to resident staff and students at all times, day and night), yielding the rough equivalent of fourteen full days; the first eight chapters passed the pre–arranged scrutiny of four independent readers (with many constructive comments) allowing the final script to reach David on time. I took the last two chapters with me to his home near Kelso at the beginning of June. It was an amazing piece of teamwork, involving many people, that enabled me to see the book published on the first morning of the Gathering under the title *Quakers in Britain: a century of change 1895-1995*. It was the only major publication marking the centenary of the Manchester Conference, and it provided the first published overview and analysis of the ways in which significant change had occurred among Quakers in Britain during this century.

Minor disability, major handicap

For most of my adult life, I have enjoyed good health, and have taken active steps to maintain general fitness. While at the Australian National University in 1969, I started regular jogging – long before it became highly popular – and kept this up for 20 years. Then osteo–arthritis in the lower back intervened, so I switched to walking exercise on a treadmill, and started swimming three times a week. I did a fair amount of walking, and used public transport as a general rule. So I reached my 79th year in pretty good shape, apart from some fairly benign heart irregularities that probably went back to the episodes in the army and afterwards, sixty years previously.

But in July 1994 I picked up an infection in my left foot which, after a fortnight of ineffective treatment at home, landed me in hospital with a cellulitis up to the knee. I was put on an intra–venous cocktail of three antibiotics which let me go home after three weeks, only to be re–admitted a fortnight later, for another couple of weeks. I was glad to be in an old fashioned 14–bed 'Nightingale ward', and although I was on 'total bed rest' could still make contact with those around me, or who were able to walk about the ward. It was a salutary experience for me. Many of the men suffered from conditions other than those which had brought them into hospital: I was next to a man of exactly my own age who suffered from angina and such poor eyesight that he could not enjoy the cricket on the television, but was also diabetic. This caused him to have several toes amputated, at intervals of about 4–6 months. After I was discharged I went up to see him, either in the house where he lived alone, or when he was back in the hospital. Eventually I was probably the last person to visit him, and was able to attend the funeral service.

The sister in charge of the ward was superb: she 'led from the front', and had created a very good team of nurses. If she was on duty at a mealtime, and not otherwise engaged, she took part in the distribution of food trays to the patients. During the six weeks of my two stays in the ward, I never saw a senior nursing officer doing a ward round, a far cry from the days when this was done daily by the matron or her deputy! In the 'modern' ward, arranged in a series of open 'rooms' with eight beds in each, plus some single–bed rooms, there is much less contact between nurses and patients, not least because many of the latter tend not to use their call–button to attract attention, except when in dire need. Yes – there are the exceptions!

I came out of this stay in hospital with my left ankle rather intolerant of weight–bearing, making desirable the use of a stick; and a 'burning toes' syndrome that affected both feet. The latter turned out to be a medical mystery, and three years later remained undiagnosed. The practical consequences were quite out of proportion to the condition, in that I became unable to stand or to walk for more than a short time, without triggering the burning/clenching sensation. This reduced my physical exercise to the regular three times/week swimming regime, and made me dependent upon my car – which fortunately I was able to drive even quite long distances. What suffered most were my domestic and gardening activities: it's surprising how much of the pruning requires one to stand up! Arthritic and other aches are dealt with by Mark, my friendly osteopath.

At about the two–year point, I decided to call upon my research experience to look into this 'burning toes' syndrome. I soon discovered that it was not uncommon in diabetes, (and among those who had experienced an attack of shingles) where it came into a medical area known as peripheral neuropathy. But fortunately I fell into neither of those categories.

Having prepared a file including my own account of my case history, a statement of my current signs and symptoms, and copies of relevant medical articles, I was fortunate to enlist the whole–hearted support of the consultant dermatologist whose clinic I attended. He referred me to the Pain Management Unit, and after exactly a year on the waiting list I found myself in the hands of an open–minded friendly team, ready to consider and to try any procedure that offered hope of relief. At the time of writing, I must simply await developments.

'Wheelchair visiting'

Since the advent of this disability, I have been able to make short trips abroad, to visit our daughter in Colorado and most of my closest friends of long-

Alastair in western Colorado, ski-ing again at 71 (on the level!) 1986

standing. These have included weekends to Lisbon and Geneva, to see Americo de Sousa and Pierre Dasen respectively, and a seven-day trip to Canada in March 1998. This arose from a very strong desire to see again my old friends Bob Logan, Sam Hershenkopf and Peter Sale, and their wives Mary, Rae and Lily.

Adding Margaret and myself, we four couples have been married for 55, 60, 59 and 57 years respectively. Despite a late heavy snowfall, I spent time with them all and was left in no doubt about what my visit meant to them. To

Alastair and Bob (1925 - 1998), Montreal, March 1998

reach the Sales in northern central Ontario, I rented a car to drive from Montreal, via Ottawa, and then south from them to Toronto (about 600 miles altogether). In Ottawa and Toronto I saw other old friends and colleagues, dating back to the middle 1950s. It was a tiring but deeply

rewarding journey, and I am glad that I was enabled to make it successfully, thanks to the staff of the wheelchair services at the airports. There is a sense of having rounded things off in a positive way.

9 Discoveries – so far

The sub–title of this book is 'A Quaker's voyage': what we have so far is an account of a very varied eighty–two years, of which I have been a Quaker for fifty–six. The approach has been largely factual, and little reference has been made to what might be called the spiritual aspects of that voyaging. To these I now turn.

Present–day Quakers in Britain are perennial seekers who frequently have difficulty in reporting what they have found. It is possible that this has as much to do with being British as with being a Quaker. They tend also to be individualists, and – most of the time – to be tolerant of other individualists. Many years ago I found myself saying that among my fellow–Quakers there was 'a premium on diffidence', that to be diffident, to avoid expressions of certainty, was a positive good, perhaps even a virtue. We are of course now thinking about matters of belief, where certainty is often hard to come by, and I do understand and respect those who find it difficult or impossible to affirm it.

Quakers do not subscribe to any theological credal statement. They do not seek authority within an ecclesiastical hierarchy. And although many even today value the Scriptures, they do not seek authority from the words of the Bible. For three hundred and fifty years, they have insisted that authority stems from direct individual and group experience of the Spirit. Until about a generation ago, most British Quakers would have agreed that they were referring to the Holy Spirit, the Spirit of the eternal Christ, 'the Light that lightens every one'. Today there is no such agreement, and diversity of personal belief has been elevated to the status of a norm. There is however a general agreement that there is something of God in every human being: unfortunately this often seems to lack meaning, through widespread inability to say what is the 'something', or what the word 'God' means to and for themselves.

I hope this short summary will be sufficient to make clear the challenge which I must take up, on the basis of my own direct experience: what have I found on the way through my life? How have I dealt with my doubts? Do I continue to be a 'seeker'?

A spiritual journey

My parents were not overtly religious, and they did not regularly attend any place of worship. I suspect that they sent me to church and Sunday School simply because it was part of my upbringing, even perhaps of my all–round education. For myself, it was not resisted, but actively enjoyed. If at the time I wondered why my parents didn't go to church, I kept this question to myself. Certainly I found the Church of Scotland emphasis on 'the Word' congenial (and fortunately not Calvinistic), and I made the most of the systematic teaching in Sunday School. So I must have reached adolescence not only free from any need to rebel or reject in religious matters, but rather with a sense of easy familiarity with the Scriptures. My selective recall suggests that my reaction to the Old Testament was fairly balanced, as between scepticism and disbelief on the one hand, and positive acceptance of, for example, the role of the prophets.

As noted earlier, during my middle teens I became interested in, and helped by, my readings in the Stoic philosophy. I think that these provided me with a respect for the exercise of wisdom and self–discipline, that complemented what I had absorbed of both Old Testament morality and 'the Christian virtues'. I do not doubt that this combination stood me in good stead as I lived through the years of unemployment, the return to Britain, my time in the Regular Army, the two long spells in hospital, and the sudden deaths of my mother and father. So the seminal challenge of the encounter with the Oxford Group then fell on prepared ground; but it also prepared me to change from a keen soldier into a conscientious objector in wartime, and then for my meeting with the Quaker movement.

How did that come about? One of the practices of the Group was to seek, at least daily, the leading of the Holy Spirit. And when the time came for me to apply for membership of the Religious Society of Friends, that application was largely based, not mainly on the importance of the peace testimony of the Society, but on my perception of the Quaker reliance on the leadings and promptings of that same Spirit. I felt that I had been led to my spiritual home, still within the Christian Church. It was as if God had said something like 'You have committed yourself to seeking my purposes for you: you will need support from others of my disciples: you will find them here'.

During the twenty years to 1963, when we left for Africa, my Quaker experience was spread across the lonely time in Italy; the close fellowship of some of the FRS team in Germany; the warmth of Wythenshawe Meeting in Manchester for seven years; two years in a meeting with internal troubles; and eight years as part of the small meeting in Heswall. Through that whole period I was mostly just an ordinary local Friend, but I think that the variety of Quaker experience provided me with basic education that was to stand me in good stead later on. So far as I can remember with any confidence, this was a process of which I was largely unaware. But the growing commitment during the five years 1958–1963, to the concern of the group that produced *Towards a Quaker view of sex*, certainly led me to seek a deepening of my spiritual life. It is probably the case that several of us came out of that experience different from what we were on entering it. For my part, I had been made to look uncomfortably closely at my own emotions, and at the values which informed but did not always govern my behaviour. More positively, I had found out through experience that the Quaker way of working within worship, to seek God's intention for the matter in hand, could lead to unexpected insights for both a group and its individual members. And I can see now how much that experience anchored and sustained me during the period of personal and family ups and downs described earlier. It also I think 'deepened' me, just ahead of the years in Zambia, without the regular support of a Quaker meeting.

That I did have in Melbourne, as once again I had to draw upon all my own spiritual resources, both at home and in the life of the university. There were many times when I might have gone under, but continued to float until things became clearer. The decision to leave Australia and return to Europe, together with the accompanying uncertainty about our longer future, was in fact not difficult. I knew what had to be done; I believed that 'way would open'; I had been prepared to put my trust in God. And that God was the same one that I had been aware of in that small room in central Italy, in 1945, who assured me that I was loved.

Following my second term at Woodbrooke College, early in 1990, I began to feel that it was time for me to see what I could learn by going on a retreat. This feeling arose naturally from my involvement in the formation of what eventually became the Quaker Retreat Group. So that August I found myself one of the two men taking part in a week–long 'guided retreat', at a Carmelite community near Tadcaster (there were eighteen women, of whom about half were lay). Apart from the daily half–hour with the 'spiritual director' to whom I had been assigned, it was entirely silent. I soon discovered ruefully that my Quaker familiarity with silence had not wholly equipped me for this: we are very good at silence – for about an hour! Fortunately, the weather was fine, so I could get out of my little room and go for walks in the surrounding countryside. My director was a Scotswoman from a small Augustinian community near Hull, Sister Jo. We 'clicked', and I have kept in touch with her – once visiting her community.

For some years, I had been using little books of daily readings, culled from the writings of Henri Nouwen and Thomas Merton. On my third morning of the retreat, the reading for that day from Merton included the following, from his book *New seeds of contemplation*:

> '**Everyone of us is shadowed by an illusory person: a false self. This is the man that I want myself to be, but who cannot exist, because God does not know anything about him.**'

I must have read those words at least twenty times in the previous three years – and had never understood what they were saying to me: that morning, I did. What a fool I was! All those years of trying to be a different person, to match the image that I had created for myself: it was time to make a fresh start, to accept my real self, the self that God knows and loves. So I did just that, during the days that followed in the retreat, and went home renewed, challenged, strengthened. New significance was given to my frequent silent use of the daily prayer of Anselm: 'Lord, what you will, where you will, when you will'. The seeker had again become a thankful finder, while remaining a seeker.

A personal theology

I hope that title does not seem arrogant – but I do think it fits what I must now attempt to do, and I wish more of my fellow–Quakers would make a similar attempt. We firmly maintain that we cannot assent to any credal statement, and therefore do not try to produce a Quaker one; it becomes a challenge to the individual. Many Quakers like to cite the question posed by the young George Fox, in Ulverston church in 1652: 'What canst thou say?'. Few of them go on with his next questions: 'Art thou a child of Light, and hast walked in the Light, and what thou speakest, is it inwardly from God?'. And of those few, how many feel able to answer 'Yes'? I know that I dare not do so without qualification: the most I can venture is 'Some of the time, and imperfectly at that'. Here is the starting point for my 'personal theology': the God that loves and chastens me also speaks to my condition, More than that, I am convinced through my own experience that God also guides and enables. That much I *can* say.

I do not pretend to understand how this comes about. And from time to time simple honesty gives rise to doubt. Yes, 'God is a spirit, and those that worship God must do so in spirit and in truth'; and faith – the willingness to trust – is of the essence. I know at first hand where that man was, who cried out 'Lord, I believe – help thou mine unbelief'. So even though it remains incomprehensible that God can and does reach out and respond to each and every one of us, I can do no other than go on trusting. Blindly? The answer would have to be 'Yes', were it not for that lifelong accumulation of experience – and the similar testimony of countless others. And where in all this do I find place for Jesus of Nazareth, for 'the risen Christ', and for the Holy Spirit? Can I call myself a Christian? Do I need a 'doctrine of the Trinity'?

Here I think is the place to say as simply and as clearly as I can what 'faith' means to me:

> **'I do not mean by "faith" any identifiable collection of specific religious beliefs. I use that word to describe the free act of placing my trust in God, when the deepest issues of my existence, my identity and my ultimate worth are at stake.**
> **I know that objective evidence or "proof" cannot be called upon to judge that action. What I am able to say arises from that trust: it does not provide the basis for it'.**

Before going further, I must explain that I have learnt to make a distinction between 'fact' and 'faith' in what I say about various topics, and to reserve my use of the expression 'I believe' for matters of faith. For example, the laws of gravity of this planet are facts, and therefore I do not say that I 'believe in them' or in their consequences. As a result my credo starts where the facts leave off, though obviously it owes a great deal to their being available. I am wholly convinced as a matter of faith – I believe, in other words – that this universe is ordered and rational and that its existence must be intentional and purposive. Nothing so intricately complex, so awe–inspiring, so beautiful could for me be accounted for in terms of pure chance or accident. So far as this planet is concerned and in particular the human species, I believe the intent to be essentially benign, or, if you like, loving. But I have been no more successful than anyone else in dealing with the 'dark side' – of natural disaster and of many diseases. I can only maintain a logical position by accepting that the creation is not 'perfect': and I find this puzzling, since it implies limitations on the attribution to God of both absolute wisdom and absolute power. Yet I remain capable of awe, and ready to worship: I am not called upon to understand what is beyond my comprehension.

Within that framework, I can believe that the benign purpose for our species included a specific freedom as individuals – and consequently as groups – to co–operate in the realisation of that purpose, or not to do so. To make such free co–operation possible, two characteristics for our species were needed: a channel through which the details of the purpose could reach the individual; and a capacity to learn from experience that contrasts sharply with the inflexibility found in, for example, the ant or the bee. These requirements were met during the evolution of our species, and I believe that my brain is the channel through which I am enabled, but not compelled, to co–operate with that benign or loving purpose.

Given the lack of compulsion even to pay attention, let alone to respond positively, it seems obvious that no rigid fore–ordained plan for either individuals or the species makes any sense. Pre–destination is not an option for me. So the benign purpose must have a completely dynamic character. Let me try to explain what I'm getting at, Just as the 'I', (myself today) is the result of the interaction between the 'I' of the day before yesterday, and my experiences and responses of yesterday, so the purpose with which I am invited to co–operate today must have needed modification, in the wake of yesterday's responses by myself and countless others. That being so, the benign purpose must in turn be infinitely modifiable.

Thought on spiritual questions is often limited by familiarity with our very useful human concepts of time and space. But there are alternative concepts, usually referred to as eternity and infinity, which provide the basis of a wholly different approach which most of us find difficult. Eternity, for example, does not mean 'for ever and ever': it is quite independent of the passage of time. But part of 'living by faith' is to be open to thinking in such alternative ways, escaping from time/space limitations.

It is also part of 'living by faith', to become and to remain prepared *not to 'know'* in the intellectual sense; to accept, for example, that not only is God beyond my capacity to describe, but that any attempt to do so simply sets up spiritual barriers. Part of my recent continuing education in spirituality has been to encounter the insights of the unknown late 14th–century local priest, in the English Midlands, who wrote *The cloud of unknowing*. He also wrote a *Letter of private direction* to a young beginner in contemplation, on the first page of which we read (in a modern translation from Middle English):

> **'Just let God be as God is. Don't try to make him anything other than he is. Don't try to penetrate his nature by clever reasoning, but base everything on faith alone'.**

To use a familiar Quaker phrase, 'that speaks to my condition', and I have accepted the direction with gratitude. That does not mean, however, that I always – or even usually – succeed in following it: mental habits of a lifetime are not shed easily.

Am I a Christian?

I must start by indicating as simply and as clearly as I can the significance to me of the historical person of Jesus. It is for me to try to answer anew what we are told was *his* question, 'Who do you say I am?'.

I shall use the religious term 'God' as shorthand, to represent all that I have earlier implied by a purpose with benign intent, which I believe gives meaning both to this ordered and rational universe and to our place in it, I can then go on to say – as part of my credo, at this present – that I also believe Jesus of Nazareth was the full expression, in terms that human beings can understand, of what that purpose implies. I further have come to believe that his death, and what has been described as his 'resurrection', were part of that full expression, and led to the formation of a fellowship of convinced men and women, through whom the process of working out God's purpose could be continued and expanded.

Here I must gladly recognise my debt to the amazing scholarship and integrity of the Swiss theologian Hans Kung. In his book *On being a Christian*, he has enabled me to achieve greater independence from familiar tradition, from the authority both of the Scriptures and of the Church, than I had been able to gain through my own inclination and efforts. Perhaps even more importantly, he has brought central issues of a theological nature into sharper focus than I had ever previously known. He is not the only Roman Catholic to whose writings I am indebted: I have already mentioned Thomas Merton and Henri Nouwen (with whom I spent a couple of hours in Toronto in 1989, and then corresponded until his untimely death in 1996).

While I do not subscribe to any concept of resurrection, which involves a coming to life again of a physical body from which life had departed, I am convinced that in some way, for which we do not have any satisfactory explanation, it was possible for a person identifiable as the familiar Jesus to appear in broad daylight to some of those who had known him before his death. I have arrived at that conviction only partly on the basis of particular statements within the Gospels, or the New Testament as a whole, partly also upon my inability to credit that the disciples would have behaved as they did, without the experiences which the New Testament reports. Here is what Paul had to say on this subject in *I Corinthians* 15 (Phillips translation):

> 'The body is sown in weakness; it is raised in power. It is sown a natural body: it is raised a spiritual body. As there is a natural body, so will there be a spiritual body .... For I assure you, my brethren, it is utterly impossible for flesh and blood to possess the kingdom of God.'

What can I say?

Am I a Christian? Using the criteria of most Christian churches, the answer must be 'No'. I am unable to assent to many of the credal statements, and I do not subscribe to the concept of a three–person Trinity (wholly absent from the New Testament) – though I do not think that makes me a unitarian, as I am about to make clear. I reject absolutely the notion that God had to be appeased by the death of Jesus, With Kung I relate to God as 'more than personal', as being one who can be addressed, and who can 'speak' to each of us. So I must identify myself as a Quaker Christian, who trusts God, is 'saved' from my self–centred wilfulness by the Inward Light of Christ, and knows that the Holy Spirit is always ready to guide and enable me, if I will but listen expectantly and be willing to follow.

When asked what 'the Inward Light' means to me, I find it difficult to better the answer given by Justin Martyr in the second century CE (as paraphrased by Henry Chadwick):

> **'Justin argues that the light that all men have is implanted by the divine Reason, the Logos of God who was incarnate in Jesus and who is universally active and present in the highest goodness and intelligence** *wherever they may be found...* **The divine Logos inspired the prophets... and was present entire in Jesus the Christ'.**

The words emphasised, with which I concur, also make me a Quaker Christian universalist – like William Penn in the 17th century, and John Woolman in the 18th, for example. Here I find it ironic that I should feel it necessary to label myself, in order to make my position clear: for many years I have held a testimony against labelling people, whether individually or as groups. The practice is potentially – and often actually – divisive, and also diverts attention away from more basic questions. For example, the most serious issue facing British Quakers is secularism, rather than whether we can be classified as either 'Christocentric' or 'Universalist'.

I cannot pretend that I have been happy to watch the membership of Britain Yearly Meeting becoming less and less representative of its 350–years Christian heritage during the last thirty years. I rejoice that we have been able to welcome many thousands as Attenders, and perhaps in that way provide each of them with a friendly and tolerant place, while they identify which is for them the right spiritual home. Though I admit to difficulty in understanding why a convinced adherent of another religious faith should feel it necessary also to become a Quaker, my universalism can cope with it. But I am unable to stretch the meaning of that term 'universalist' to cover the position of those who insist that they are agnostic or atheist. That is not to criticize or judge them – far from it: I wish for them the best that I know myself, and pray that they will be reached inwardly by the Light. If and when that happens, they can be shown the way that is right – for each of them as individual children of God – which will not necessarily be the one that has proved 'right' for me.. As Jesus said 'In my Father's house there are many mansions'.

So I have been just another seeker, who has made some findings, and gone on seeking still. Quakers are encouraged to 'be open to fresh light, from whatever source it may arise': I try to live that way. But I have learned the necessity of putting what appears to be 'fresh light' to the test of spiritual discernment, my own and that of others. And I am well aware that I do not always 'get it right'. But I've always enjoyed living adventurously.

Retrospective

I retired – for the last time, and completely – halfway through my eighty–second year. It meant in practice that I ceased to hold office, or to serve on any committee, Quaker or other, while remaining available for 'one–off' or other short–term service. I'd had a good run for my money, and a very great deal for which to feel deeply thankful. So the time has come to attempt something a bit like an end of term self–report.

Although my home life as a child and adolescent had some obvious drawbacks, much was positive. I learned to adapt, eventually without effort, to new situations – to six primary schools, for example. I reached my early thirties before my stay in the same abode exceeded about two years. My mother equipped me with domestic skills and a feeling of complete equality with women; my father with a living demonstration of accepted duty, whatever the circumstances. Their values were broadly consistent with those I encountered in church and Sunday school, and in most of my teachers.

Although my school education would until very recently be seen as old–fashioned and too formal, it has served me well, sending me out literate, numerate, scientifically–oriented but with a real interest in literature and history.

I have one major regret: that there was no opportunity for me to become even a modest amateur with a musical instrument, to enlighten and enrich my early and sustained appreciation of music. When I was about seventeen, in Montreal, one Sunday I found myself listening to a concert broadcast from New York – and the music was that of Beethoven's fifth symphony. Like countless others I was at once enthralled, bowled over in fact! So I started listening regularly to the weekly 'music appreciation hour', conducted and presented by Walter Damrosch; to opera from 'the Met'; and then to both Stokowski with the Philadelphia Symphony Orchestra, and Toscanini with the New York – under whom I first heard the Beethoven *Missa Solennis*. All this laid the foundation for lifelong interest in and appreciation of serious music. By twenty–one I had reached already the point when I could wait at the stage door of the Queen's Hall in London, to say 'Thank you' as she came out to the 'pocket soprano' Lily Pons – for which I got a friendly smile and a nod of the head.

In addition to my trio of early close friends (Bob, Sam, and Peter), I have valued the friendship of many whom I met during my stays in various places around the world, and with whom I have managed to keep in touch even if only through a yearly newsletter. But I am especially thankful for what I can only think of as a privilege: the enduring friendship – even love – of several men and women from the same age–group as my own children. This has done much to make up for the dismaying experience of finding all too often that people experience me as daunting. Some of those have persevered, allowing me time and opportunity to demolish my unwanted pedestal. Although I have often been described as 'a good listener', it does not always make up for my spoken fluency, or my tendency to sound just too confident for the comfort of others. Though I suspect the origins of this lie right back in my schooldays, when I had only my tongue to 'fight with', I have never felt this excused it. That this characteristic has often led to the withholding of full acceptance by many of my fellow–Quakers, including those in my local meeting, I have gradually learned to live with, though I must admit to some sadness.

What I learned to do about it arose directly from my faith. For most of my adult life I have recognised that I could not change myself, but must instead pray constantly to be changed by an inward gift of grace. Some of my close friends from time to time provided indications that this prayer has been answered – to the extent that I have cooperated in the process. My now–settled aim is to become, in Merton's words, 'the person that God knows about'.

But in terms of ordinary everyday living, I owe most to the love and forbearance of my wife and equal partner for more than fifty–seven years. The foundations for that partnership were deeply spiritual. We both believed that God had brought us together; that if we each stayed willing and open, what needed to change in us could be changed. To use an old–fashioned saying, we felt that our marriage was 'made in Heaven', and understood why the formal ceremony did but solemnise publicly what was already a full commitment, based on mutual sharing with no holds barred, and a determination 'never to let the sun go down on your wrath'. In the love of God, and with the support of our family and friends, we have been enabled to surface from the worst and go on to enjoy the better. It has been for me a lived experience that 'where God guides, God also provides'.

Here too I want to give thanks for our son Keith and our daughter Joy. Although they have been an essential part of my story, I have refrained from telling their stories for them. Like us, they have experienced their downs and ups, and are now enjoying their mature years. Keith spent the whole of his thirty–one years of full–time employment with the National Health Service, retiring when yet another re–organisation broke up the district of which he had been the foundation general manager. His skills in the computer domain now combine with his administrative experience as the basis for home–based consultancy. Joy in mid–life took a year off from nursing to qualify as a Certified Nurse Midwife, and shares a flourishing practice with her colleague in western Colorado. Margaret and I have four grandchildren and two great–grandchildren.

For myself, I respect, admire and love both our children. In their different ways and circumstances they have both displayed patience, courage and a positive spirit. They are people with whom it is easy to relate. As a father, I have got much better than I deserved: two good friends.

No one ever achieves complete insight (not even with the help of a training and experience in psychology). But I want to end this Quaker's story with a brief self–evaluation. Intellectually I have never been 'top drawer', just a pretty adequate 'upper–second'. It does not stretch the truth to describe me as a 'Jack of all trades and master of none', a sort of all–rounder. The shifts of emphasis in my scientific and professional career were frequent enough and significant enough to ensure that I never became famous, which is probably just as well! A vice–chancellor friend astutely observed about thirty years ago that I was probably the best administrator he knew, though not much of a diplomat. Perhaps my greatest asset has been the gift of an inveterate problem–solving attitude, whether to a practical difficulty in my home or workshop, or to a seemingly insoluble situation. And I enjoy challenges — like giving myself a computer as a present on my seventieth birthday!

Though of course others should judge, I do not recall any period in which I felt my commitment to the task or situation was less than whole–hearted. Perhaps my best spells were those in Zambia, Australia and Sheffield, both in terms of my own feelings about them, and what others were generous in expressing. I am very glad about the success of the pre–retirement education movement in Britain, and grateful for the flexibility shown by the PRA as it extended its work to mid–life preparation in recent years. In my life as a Quaker, though my writings seem to have been generally welcome but rarely quoted, I may perhaps be remembered at least as much for the contribution that I was able to make to the creation of a modern meeting house in the heart of my adopted city of Sheffield. So on balance this 'one life' may have been serviceable – and I wouldn't have missed it for all the tea in China!